Lever House

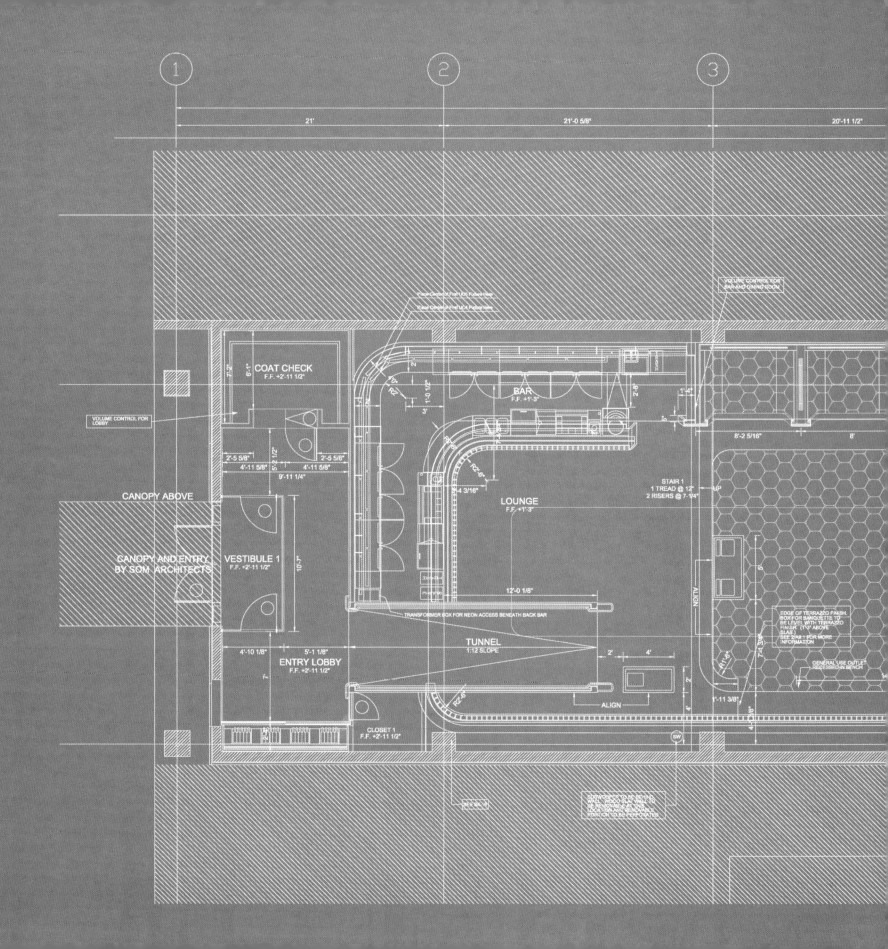

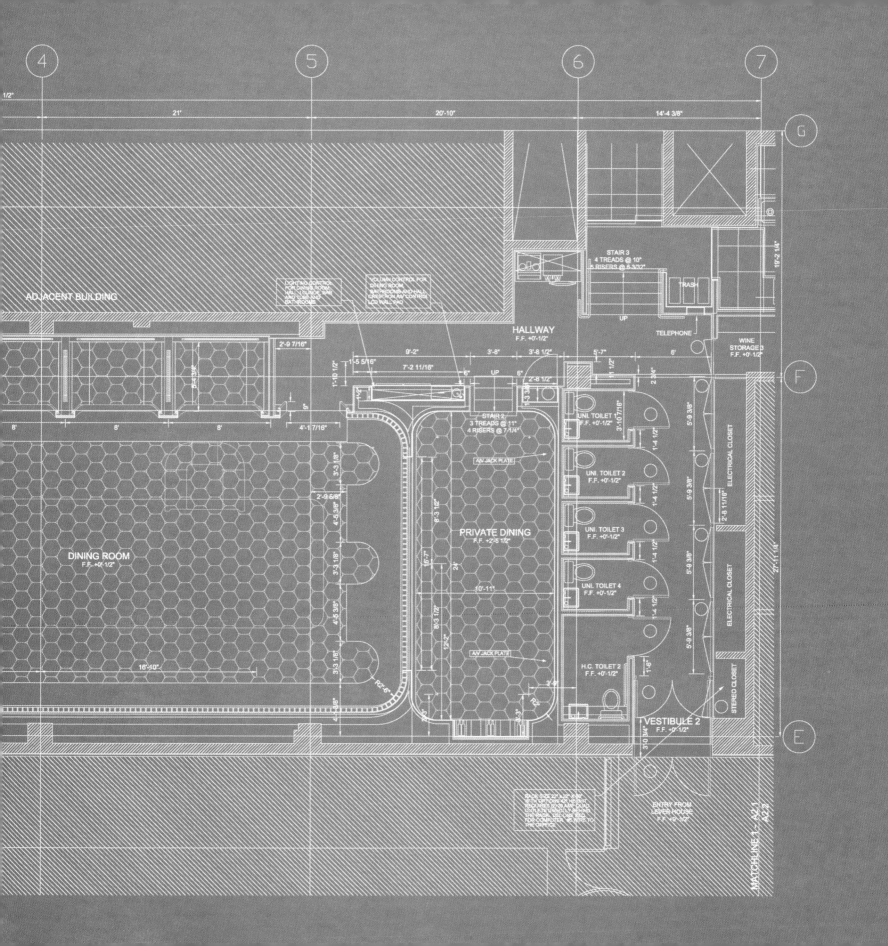

Lever House

THE LEVER HOUSE COOKBOOK

DAN SILVERMAN & JOANN CIANCIULLI
INTRODUCTION BY MATT TYRNAUER
PHOTOGRAPHS BY ROBERTO D'ADDONA

CLARKSON POTTER/PUBLISHERS
NEW YORK

Published in the United States by Clarkson Potter/Publishers, an imprint of

the Crown Publishing Group, a division of Random House, Inc., New York.

www.crownpublishing.com

www.clarksonpotter.com

Clarkson N. Potter is a trademark and Potter and colophon

are registered trademarks of Random House, Inc.

Library of Congress Cataloging-in-Publication Data

Silverman, Dan.

The Lever House cookbook / Dan Silverman and JoAnn Cianciulli. Includes index.

1. Cookery.   2. Lever House (New York, N.Y.)   I. Cianciulli, JoAnn.   II. Title.

TX714.S573   2005

641.5—dc22   2005016621

ISBN-13: 978-1-4000-9780-7

ISBN-10: 1-4000-9780-0

Printed in China

Design by Level, Calistoga, CA

10 9 8 7 6 5 4 3 2 1

First Edition

FOR SUSAN AND GEORGIA

contents

THE GLASS HOUSE BY MATT TYRNAUER

Lever House is often called one of the greatest buildings of the twentieth century. New York's first all-glass International Style skyscraper, a bottle-green–colored gem, made Le Corbusier's and Mies van der Rohe's dreams of thin-skinned, lightweight glass–and-steel towers a reality. Its meticulous restoration and rebirth, which includes John McDonald and Josh Pickard's Lever House Restaurant, designed with spare jet-age elegance by Marc Newson, and tucked discretely into the space where the old Lever Brothers corporate auditorium once was, has been a genuine cause for celebration in Manhattan since its opening in 2003.

In 1952, the last year of Harry S. Truman's administration, a year when only 3 percent of the American public traveled by plane, and only 34 percent had TV sets, Lever House seemed as though it had dropped from the sky all in one piece onto Park Avenue across from McKim, Mead, and White's Racquet and Tennis Club. Its glass and stainless-steel slabs—one horizontal set over columns on an open ground floor, and another vertical perched as if floating above it—were unlike anything anyone had seen before. By day, the structure shimmered in the sunlight and reflected the façade of the brick and limestone Montana Apartments across Park Avenue. By night it lit up like a taut rectangular lantern—a vision of the future on a block between 53rd and 54th streets. For weeks after the building opened its doors in April, curious citizens lined up to enter its spare, glass-enclosed lobby for a closer look. So many arrived to see the place that the elevator systems, designed to handle only the 1,200 employees of the Lever Brothers Corporation and a normal flow of visitors, came close to breaking down. The architecture critic Lewis Mumford noted that the public was acting as if a new soap company headquarters was "the eighth wonder of the world."

In a way, you could not blame them. Two decades of economic hardship and war had recently drawn to a close. In those years no significant buildings (with the exception of Rockefeller Center) were constructed in New York. But now the American economy was gearing up, and Modernism, at last, was about to take hold in the U.S.

The heroes of this story of avant-garde design are an unlikely bunch. They are not the

kind of people who wore round glasses with thick black horn rims or spoke with heavy German accents. Lever House was an all-American venture. It was the work of a then-obscure architecture firm called Skidmore, Owings & Merrill (now one of the world's largest) and its chief designer, Gordon Bunshaft, who in the fifties and sixties was to become a key player—perhaps *the* key player—in the transformation of European Modernist architecture from its beginnings as a radical style with roots in socialism, to its ultimate destiny as the style of corporate America and the American Century.

The firm of Skidmore, Owings & Merrill (S.O.M.) was founded in 1936 by friends and in-laws Louis Skidmore (1897–1962) and Nathaniel Owings (1903–1984). Skidmore, known as "Skid," was married to Owings's sister, Eloise. John Merrill (1896–1975), an engineer, was brought into the partnership in 1939, but played a relatively minor role, despite having his name on the door. The original office was opened in Chicago, but Skidmore moved almost immediately to New York, where he was engaged as a consultant for the 1939 World's Fair.

Working out of a small studio at 5 East 57th Street, Skidmore and a few associates churned out designs for fair pavilions for companies such as Heinz, Wonder Bread, and Westinghouse. Such small-scale corporate commissions would later yield important business for the firm, most notably from Heinz, for whom S.O.M. designed buildings in the U.S. and England. (In an instance of aesthetic enlightenment winning out over business instincts, it was Skidmore who managed to talk H.J. Heinz II out of placing a huge neon pickle on top of his S.O.M.-designed vinegar factory in Pittsburgh.)

Both Skidmore and Owings were smooth, charismatic club men who moved easily in the world of the WASP business establishment. What the partners were not known for was their talent as designers. From the very beginning they depended on those they hired to do the creative work, and most of the time they did not even bother to lift a pencil. Natalie de Blois, an architect in S.O.M.'s New York office in the early years, recalls that Skidmore "sat in the conference room, at the end of the conference

table, and talked on the telephone. You know, he wasn't ever near a drafting board." Owings, a colleague once commented, "couldn't draw water." The partners compensated for their lack of artistic ability with keen rain-making skills, organizational talent, and a certain visionary flair. Like the corporate chieftains with whom they got on so well, Skidmore and Owings were entrepreneurial, had sharp marketing instincts, and were unafraid to bet on expansion. These were unusual traits for architects of the era around the Second World War,

when most firms were structured as small ateliers. "Until the war, most U.S. architects were trained to work only on small [jobs]," Skidmore told a reporter from *Fortune* magazine, in a 1952 article called "The Architects From Skid's Row." "They left the problems of coping with large scale projects—industrial plants, airfields—to the engineer. We felt that the architect would have to win back the role of creator and coordinator of big projects."

This brand of gumption paid off in a big way when World War II arrived, and S.O.M. was awarded a major government project for the design of the 75,000-person "secret atomic town" of Oak Ridge, Tennessee, home of the Manhattan Project.

In 1937, Skidmore made what would prove to be the best hire of his life.

Twenty-eight-year-old Gordon Bunshaft, a graduate of MIT, showed up at the 57th Street office with a stack of photographs he had taken while in Europe on a prestigious travel award called the Rotch Fellowship. Skidmore (who had also won the Rotch), saw promise in the young man, whose only previous experience had been a few months with the fledgling practice of Edward Durrell Stone, and a few months in the office of the industrial designer Raymond Loewy. Bunshaft liked Stone, but was not fond of Loewy; he once told an interviewer Loewy was a "phony" who would "put a gold line on a cigarette or on a railroad train, and he'd get a fee for it." Later, the animosity would continue, when Loewy (who created soap packaging for Lever Brothers) was hired to design the interiors of Lever House, including the auditorium where the restaurant now sits. Over time, all of Loewy's streamlined interiors were ripped out and replaced, except for the executive offices on the top floor, which remain intact to this day, and serve as proof of Bunshaft and Loewy's aesthetic differences. The dark wood and fireplaces on this floor clash mightily with the cool glass exterior. Everyone would agree that Bunshaft won the test of time.

If social adeptness and bonhomie defined Skidmore and Owings, Bunshaft was their opposite. This made them a good team, with Bunshaft functioning as Mr. Inside—the firm's secret design weapon—and the two name partners functioning as Messrs. Outside. (Owings once said that the name of the firm should have

been changed to Skidmore, Owings & Bunshaft, but that never happened because the resulting initials would then have been S.O.B.)

Bunshaft's rough demeanor is the stuff of legend in architectural circles. As Brendan Gill wrote in his 1990 obituary of Bunshaft in *The New Yorker*: "[He] was . . . so grumpily taciturn that close friends seeking to provide a kindly description of him would often fall back upon the adjective 'difficult.'"

In one of his last interviews, Philip Johnson, the late dean of American architects, told me that Bunshaft "could be mean and gruff, until I got to know him, and then I became a tremendous admirer and a great friend. But that was towards the end. Before, when we were both working on Lincoln Center, we used to scream at each other. I remember I apologized to him. I said, 'Bun, I have screamed at you a lot, and *you* haven't been so nice.' He returned the apology, because after he'd scream, he'd feel bad. He was a good soul. But I never did know why he was so gruff. It would be nice to find the key, wouldn't it?"

More than likely, according to people who knew him, Bunshaft was crippled by what he

perceived to be his various deficiencies—social, physical, and otherwise. He had a chip on his shoulder, which some observers felt arose from insecurities about being overweight and rather short, and, though he never discussed it, being Jewish. Architecture, in the middle of the last century, was still a WASP preserve. One of his colleagues told me that Bunshaft had been blackballed from the prestigious artistic and literary society the Century Club, "and he knew who'd done this to him." He bore the slight for life.

At one point, Bunshaft's religion worked in his favor. When S.O.M. was under consideration for the Lever House job, the C.E.O. of Lever Brothers at the time was Charles Luckman, who was Jewish. Bunshaft recalled that Skidmore and Owings brought him to a meeting with Luckman at the Lever Brothers' apartment in the Waldorf Towers. "Skid and Nat took me along because they . . . thought . . . Luckman might think me compatible, or Luckman, being Jewish, might think I'm Jewish or something," Bunshaft said. "But I didn't say a damn thing in the meeting."

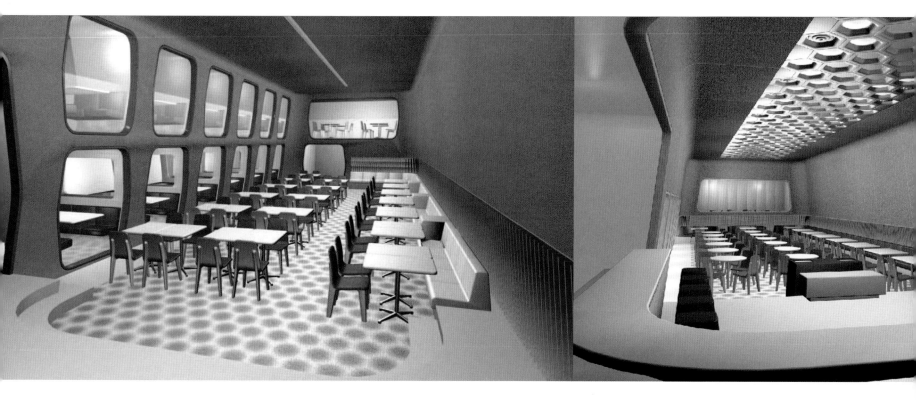

Luckman was the right client at the right time for S.O.M. Trained as an architect, he went into the soap business during the Great Depression, and rose to the top of Lever Brothers by the time he was thirty-seven. He was determined to commission a building that would enhance the company's prestige and increase its public profile. Thus, Lever House would become the first of a great generation of iconic Modern corporate buildings in New York City. (Later examples of this genre include the Pepsi-Cola building at 500 Park Avenue;

the Union Carbide Building, now J.P. Morgan Chase, at 270 Park Avenue; the Chase Manhattan Building near Wall Street—all by Bunshaft —the CBS Building on 6th Avenue by Eero Saarinen; and the Seagram Building, across from Lever House, at 375 Park Avenue, by Mies van der Rohe with Philip Johnson.)

Perhaps the most unusual aspect of the program Luckman put forward for Lever House was that the building was not to use the full amount of square footage allowed by New York City's building codes. (In fact, it uses only

half of the space allowed by law.) This was an extraordinary act of philanthropy on Lever's part, which resulted in a building of modest density with a great deal of open airspace around it.

The form Bunshaft chose for Lever House was simple. Inspired by Le Corbusier's Swiss Pavilion in Paris, he put the building on stilts, raising the horizontal slab—which is a block long and defines the Park Avenue building line —above an open ground-floor plaza. The tall, slender, vertical slab, positioned at a right angle to Park Avenue, rises twenty-two stories and is set off-center. This allows for a 50-foot-square courtyard in the middle of the "floating" *piano nobile*. It also permits the courtyard and one side of the tower to receive sunlight from the south, over the top of the six-story Racquet Club building across the street. Because the Lever tower covers only 25 percent of the site, it is allowed by zoning laws to rise without wedding-cake setbacks. This was highly unusual for the time.

The ground floor of the building consists of only a garden set in the courtyard and the glass-enclosed lobby, underneath the tower,

near the north of the block. This "open plan" works well with Bunshaft's Corbusian scheme, but was also very much a part of Luckman's PR scheme for the building. He rightly determined that the publicity Lever would get by allowing pedestrians access to open gardens on Park Avenue would be far more valuable than the profits the company would make from renting ground-floor space to retail stores or a bank. He also did not want the building to be identified with anything other than Lever Brothers.

No one, including Skidmore, could believe that the building would be approved by the Lever Brothers board of directors without stores planned for the ground floor. Just before Bunshaft presented the final design to Luckman, Skidmore suggested to him that he make a model with shops on the bottom. As Bunshaft once recounted in an interview, "Skid said, 'You'll never get away without stores. It's crazy.' I said, 'Well, it's the whole goddamn design.' He said, 'You've got to put in stores.' So, I put them in and Luckman came over. . . . He said, 'What happened to it? What's that stuff in the bottom, Skidmore?' He said 'Stores. You've got to have them.' He said, 'You've ruined the

whole design.' If he'd have gone along with that, the building would have been nothing." Luckman's plan was soft-sell advertising (not to mention corporate branding) brought to a new level of sophistication. As Lewis Mumford wrote in his review of the building in *The New Yorker*, "This whole structure is chastely free of advertisement; the minuscule glass cases showing life-size packages of Lever products in the glass-enclosed reception chamber on the ground floor would hardly be noticed in the lobby of a good hotel. But the building itself is a showcase and an advertisement; in its very avoidance of vulgar forms of publicity, it has become one of the most valuable pieces of advertising a big commercial enterprise could conceive."

At the time Lever House opened, the only other building in New York with a glass window wall was the United Nations Secretariat (dedicated in 1951, and designed by Wallace K. Harrison, Le Corbusier, and Oscar Niemeyer, with an international consortium of architects). Lever House and the U.N. are related in principle, but there are major differences—the most dramatic of which is that Lever House is wrapped by glass on all sides (except for part of the west wall, which is a brick service core), whereas the U.N. is glass on only two sides. In addition, the windows at the U.N. are not sealed. Bunshaft and S.O.M. were involved peripherally in the design of the U.N., and De Blois, who worked on Lever House, recalls that "After spending some time with Wally Harrison and the U.N. group, Gordon was inspired. The window wall was very much under discussion. It was in the air, and I remember sitting with Gordon on my right, and some other people, and him saying, 'Well, this is what we're going to go with. We are going to make it all glass. We're going to have glass windows *and* glass spandrels. The whole thing was going to be glass.'"

Ever since Mies van der Rohe had drawn proposals for monumental glass-walled skyscrapers in the 1920s, long before they were technically feasible, the dream of a glazed tower had been alive. Le Corbusier had experimented with glass curtain walls on a small scale, most famously—and disastrously—at the Salvation Army Hostel (1933) in Paris, where the south-facing glass

façade turned the un-air-conditioned dormitory into an avant-garde toaster oven. By mid-century, industrial-strength air-conditioning systems, as well as heat-absorbing glass and cooler fluorescent lighting, finally made the glass tower a possibility. It is interesting to note that Bunshaft, an indirect disciple of Le Corbusier and Mies, beat the two masters at their own game, pushing the limits of technology far enough to get the glass wall built before anyone else. In later years, Bunshaft confessed that he and his partners were in the dark as to how to make the glass stay in place on the building. Only after months of extensive research by outside engineers and contractors was it determined that it could be done.

Despite various criticisms over the years, Lever House has always been viewed by architects and historians as a watershed for architecture in the U.S. "It gave architectural expression to an age just as the age was being born," the art critic Reyner Banham wrote. "And while the age lasted, or its standard persisted, Lever House was an uncontrollable success, imitated and sometimes understood all over the Americanized world, and one of the sights of New York." It was the first building ever to receive New York City landmark designation at the minimum age of thirty. At that time, Bunshaft became the only living architect with a New York City landmark building to his name. The same year, 1982, was also a nearly fatal one for Lever, as a developer bought the land underneath the building and attempted to tear it down. A Save Lever movement was hastily formed—led, in part, by Jacqueline Kennedy Onassis and Philip Johnson. The building was preserved after the New York City Board of Estimate ratified the landmark designation in a five-to-four vote.

Five years ago, the ownership of Lever House changed again, when developer Aby Rosen bought the building and started a careful restoration. Lever Brothers has vacated all but the top four floors, and Rosen (who also owns the Seagram Building across the street) has brought in new tenants such as Alcoa and Providence Equity. When Rosen took over, he promised the Landmarks Preservation Commission that he would restore the building's curtain wall, which had been decaying steadily due to structural defects. Sixty million dollars later, in addition to a gleaming new exterior, the building's street-level garden has been redone, and now includes several 1950s period sculptures by Isamu Noguchi. Originally, Bunshaft had commissioned Noguchi to design landscaping and sculptures for the plaza, but he was unable to complete the project.

Another goal of Rosen's was to open a restaurant that would "inject life into the building in a similar way that the Four Seasons and the Brasserie do to the Seagram Building," says John McDonald. Rosen's original plan was to build the restaurant in the third floor of the tower (site of the former Lever employee cafeteria, designed by Loewy), which opens out onto the roof of the horizontal slab, where Lever employees once played shuffleboard. He had a fantasy about outdoor, rooftop dining overlooking Park Avenue. This fantasy was not shared by the Landmarks Commission.

Plan B: The old auditorium, a windowless

space that could be accessed from an entrance on 53rd Street. Rosen turned to McDonald and Josh Pickard, veteran restaurateurs, each with several successful Manhattan establishments to their name. (The partners also own Lure Fishbar and Chinatown Brasserie.)

McDonald had worked with the Australian-born Marc Newson, one of the foremost industrial designers of the present day, on the interior of Canteen, and it was without hesitation that he turned to Newson for ideas about how to build a new high-profile restaurant in a landmark Modern building—a restaurant that would complement the iconic Four Seasons in Rosen's Seagram Building, but not mimic it.

"I really wanted to use Marc, because I knew that he would not go backwards," says McDonald. "I could just envision the conversations that I would have had with other architects, about how they were going to create a perfect 1950s look and re-create the genre. How do you re-create what's across the street, which was designed by Philip Johnson and is perfect? I would never have even *entertained* it. You respect and leave the history of what they did on its own."

Newson agrees. "It would have been futile, you know? But our primary objective was to create our own landmark, because we understood the significance of Lever House from a historical perspective, and I was very interested in honoring the building. Having said that, I tried very hard not to get too bogged down in the iconography of Lever House. I thought that, on one hand, what I needed to do was to be sympathetic to the exterior. But I didn't feel that the interior should be in any way like the exterior, because then you run risk that it's kind of competing, and it wouldn't be very easy to compete with that."

Newson, who has offices in London and Paris, set out to design something that had its own character: "Different," he says, "in a fundamental way, but similar enough so they could sort of live together."

Once again, an industrial designer was charged with making an important interior contribution to Bunshaft's Lever House, and, like Loewy, Newson's instinct was to play the interior design against the cool and rigid exterior of the building.

While taking a tour of the building with Rosen, Newson noted that some of the surviving Loewy floors contained a lot of wood. He also admired one original wall in the lobby, "a sort of glass ceramic tile wall," which he says he "found to be one of the most beautiful parts of the whole place."

The restaurant, which sits in a large oblong shoe box of a space, slightly below grade, was built with a limited palette of materials: terrazzo, Japanese-teahouse plaster, ceramic, leather, Australian oak, and Corian, a DuPont synthetic that mimics stone such as alabaster. The colors are mostly browns, tans, and grays, lit to give off a warm glow. Material and tone are not the only way the interior design contrasts with the exterior. As opposed to the building's taut geometry, almost every surface in the dining room has a soft curve. Avid followers of Newson's work will not be surprised to find this: curves are a trademark, best exemplified by his famous Lockheed lounge chair, a bulbous, highly polished aluminum chaise, which is riveted together, evoking the skin of a Lockheed Electra fuselage.

To prepare visitors for the jump-cut from bottle-green International Style Lever House on 53rd Street to Newson's Lever House, the designer placed a people-sized white Corian tube between the entrance vestibule and the dining room, a sort of symbolic passageway which has, in McDonald's words, "a transporting feel."

"When people walk down the tube, you hear them say that it reminds them of the Eero Saarinen tubes at the JFK TWA terminal," McDonald adds. The room on the street side of the passage (where you check your coat, and where wine is stored behind walls of glass) is made of black granite, matching the ground-floor exterior wall of the building on 53rd Street. After you hit the Corian, you are in another world with its own kind of precision and perfection—a large dining room unobstructed by pillars, and with no windows, unless you count the large rectangular one that allows you to see into the private dining room at the rear of the restaurant, and permits the private diners to overlook the scene of the big room. The feeling is part sci-fi/part retro-fifties, as if a NASA engineer had been charged with designing a dining room at the United Nations, or as if Saarinen were still alive

and working with space-age polymers. "I was thinking in terms of that era; that's where I drew from," says Newson, referring to the Saarinen aesthetic and the time of big glamorous jet-age transportation projects. Newson also looked farther afield, toward "something like the Okura Hotel in Tokyo," designed in 1962 by Yoshiro Taniguchi, the father of Yoshio Taniguchi, architect of the new addition to the Museum of Modern Art in New York.

If you were going to compare Bunshaft's design vision to Newson's, you might find one common ground: the concept of seamlessness. One of Bunshaft's goals was to make perfect curtain walls in an era when Modernists wanted buildings to appear machine-made. Newson, who was trained as a silversmith à la Georg Jensen, also has seamlessness at the front of his mind, although a more curvaceous brand. Corian, for example, can be molded into any shape, so the entry tube is one perfectly smooth trapezoidal unit. There is also a great feeling of smooth modularity to the elaborate ceramic lighting unit embedded in the dining room's ceiling. Rectangular and honeycomb shaped, it looks like something you might dream of finding in the dining room of a great Zeppelin. (Honeycomb shapes are also echoed in the bar area, a few steps up from the dining room at the front of the restaurant. Here the combs are etched into the mirrored walls.) There are very few right angles in the restaurant—even the plaster walls curve at the ceiling, like an organic membrane encasing the room.

"Making something seamless is always far more complex than it looks," says Newson. "A lot of engineering goes into making it look simple." If Bunshaft and Newson were to have a conversation (departing from the metaphysical design dialogue between their separate Lever House projects), they would probably agree to disagree on many things—if only because Bunshaft was famously dismissive of other designers, especially younger ones. But on the last concept of making the complex seem simple, they would surely be of exactly the same mind.

Lever House

LEVER HOUSE FOOD PHILOSOPHY

When I started thinking about the menu and food for Lever House, I often thought about Marc Newson's stunning restaurant design and wondered how I would be able to compete. The more I thought about it, the more difficult my goal seemed. Then I thought, why compete? Why not just make really flavorful food, focus on great ingredients, and let them speak for themselves?

The food at Lever House is seasonal, well-sourced, fresh, and delicious. It isn't complicated or contrived. Because what we do is so seemingly simple, we place a great deal of emphasis on quality, technique, and timing. Only some of our dishes call for a lot of ingredients. In fact, many ingredient lists are relatively short. If we're making a lamb dish or a scallop dish, everything on the plate should be working to help that main ingredient pop. When developing new menu ideas, the question I ask myself most frequently isn't, What does this dish need? It's more likely, What can I remove? For us, the fewer the ingredients, the cleaner and more articulate the flavors. For example, if the tuna we get isn't beautiful, then our tuna carpaccio wouldn't be as good as it is. If we didn't

painstakingly experiment with the balance of the sauce—a simple combination of crème fraîche, wasabi, ginger, and lime juice—and apply it judiciously to the tuna, we would have just another tuna carpaccio, one of hundreds in New York. Ours stands out because we begin with the best ingredients we can find, and work to fine-tune the plate until it really sings.

At the restaurant, we are constantly searching for products coming into season, hard-to-find ingredients or unusual items I think our guests will enjoy. Since we are located on Park Avenue in the heart of Midtown Manhattan and since I've been cooking for many years and have developed and cultivated relationships with a wide array of farmers, butchers, fishmongers, fruit and vegetable vendors, this isn't quite as difficult as it sounds. In fact, it is one of the more educational and fun parts of my job as a chef. I can learn more talking to a fisherman, farmer, or butcher about their respective product in ten minutes than I might in reading an essay about it. Don't get me wrong, I also draw inspiration from combing scads of books and magazines about food, as well as dining out all over the country. I enjoy talking to my

BY DAN SILVERMAN

purveyors because they have interesting and informative stories to tell and because they are all very passionate about what they do.

Although the recipes in this book were conceived as fully realized dishes, you shouldn't feel that substitutions are out of the question. That is to say, if you look through the book and decide to make the halibut, but find when shopping that the halibut looks old and tired yet the fluke or the bass look like they were just plucked from the water, I say improvise. Take advantage of what's best.

In addition, think about who you are cooking for and why. These recipes are the way we serve the dishes in the restaurant, but feel free not only to mix and match but also to omit a recipe component if you have time constraints. Do, however, follow the measurements of the given recipes, as the ratios of ingredients have been calibrated for optimum flavor.

I am proud that so many people make the conscious decision to dine at Lever House. Some are joining us for the first time and some for the hundredth. Some come to do business, others for pleasure. Whatever the reason, they have all made a choice. I try to do everything

in my power to make them happy. After all, next time they have to choose where to eat, I would be thrilled if they chose us again! Whether trying to accommodate someone with a food allergy, devising a tasting menu for a special occasion, or substituting one fish for another, I think that cooking for other people is a loving act. When everything works right, being a chef is a really special job. Going out into the dining room and seeing people enjoy the things that I've come up with is truly satisfying.

At Lever House, we serve grown-up, clear-headed food that is elegant without being too fussy. It is my sincere hope that this book captures the cuisine and I encourage you to enjoy the recipes at home.

A WORD OR TWO ABOUT SALT AND SEASONING

Salt and pepper are two of the most important ingredients in my kitchen. A good steak that isn't seasoned with salt and pepper is just a piece of meat. Seasoned with salt and pepper, cooked to perfection, and then sprinkled with a bit more salt to finish it off, the steak is elevated to a higher level. When seasoning raw steak, or any uncooked food for that matter, you should actually see the seasoning on it, even if you can't taste it directly.

My affection for salt and pepper runs deep. I am a longtime lover of anchovies, capers, and soy sauce. All of these ingredients offer a different type of salinity—when added to a braise or sauce, anchovies add a deep understated note; capers seem somehow more exclamatory, bursting in your mouth with a pungent and vegetal tang; while soy can be mellow and almost winy.

Chilies fresh and dried have different levels of fruitiness as well as heat. Some fresh chilies —serranos and Thai chilies—are immediately hot and then dissipate quickly, while others are milder yet linger longer on the palate. One of my favorites, Aleppo pepper, has a deliciously deep flavor that is hotter than paprika yet milder than cayenne and seems to work well with a lot of the food we cook at Lever House.

Remember to taste food constantly through the cooking process. Seasoning is not about measuring; it's about tasting as you go and layering salt and pepper in stages to build flavor. Whether you are preparing a simple salad or a complex and lengthy braise—season when you begin, cook, taste, season, cook some more, taste again, season, and then just before serving taste and adjust the seasoning. As long as you season in judicious additions, you shouldn't ever have to worry about overseasoning.

I know that some people choose not to use salt for reasons of health. Some people choose not to use pepper or chilies because they don't like "spicy" food. The food at Lever House is neither salty nor spicy, it is well seasoned. One reason it is as good as it is (I hope), besides the care we take in sourcing and preparing it, is our constant and consistent attention to seasoning. If you do have health issues that prohibit or proscribe the use of salt, then please feel free to omit the salt when preparing the recipes in this book.

VINAIGRETTE VIGNETTE

Vinaigrettes are easy to assemble, they hold well, and they are bright and vibrant. They can be simple or complex, and they are versatile, flexible, and varied—use them to dress a salad, marinate fish, or serve as a sauce.

Restaurant kitchens are not known for having lots of elbow room, and burner and oven space are valuable commodities. There is often a similar problem at home. Whether you're preparing an informal family meal or making a more involved dinner for friends, vinaigrettes can be lifesavers. I like vinaigrettes as sauces because they are light, providing a vivid blast of flavor that a traditional sauce cannot deliver. Plus, they can be prepared ahead, which is a real time-saver. I'm not down on sauces, though. In fact, I think the ability to make well-balanced, flavorful, and correct sauces is a dying art. Whether preparing a classic sauce or a vinaigrette, there is no substituting for taste. Taste your sauce or vinaigrette frequently as you create. Adjust as you see fit. An underseasoned or poorly balanced sauce or vinaigrette will mar an otherwise well-prepared dish. Also, be sure you taste the sauce or vinaigrette on the food before you serve it.

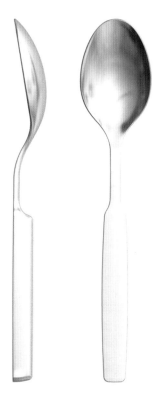

RAW RECIPES

The raw items on the menu at Lever House feature the freshest fish and meats that we can find. A succulent plate of raw yellowtail hamachi or yellowfin tuna can be revelatory. A plate of tuna of questionable age will at best be average, lacking bright color and flavor. As with salads, don't drown the fish (or meat) with dressings or garnishes. These accents should serve as highlights and not as distractions from the main event.

It pays to develop a relationship with a local fishmonger. I am constantly on the lookout for new purveyors who can get me fresher product. I am happy that I've been able to source live langoustines from Scotland and local fluke that is less than a day old!

WHITE TUNA TARTARE WITH CRÈME FRAÎCHE AND CAPERS SERVES 4

Albacore tuna is truly the other white meat. Also known as Tombo in Hawaii, the fish is remarkably buttery uncooked. Cut the tuna in a large dice so you can experience the meltingly tender quality of the fish. It's always best to use excellent extra-virgin olive oil, and the finest quality is never more important than on this tuna tartare. At the restaurant, we use Nuñez de Prado Spanish olive oil because it is 100 percent organic with very low acidity. The floral essences of this unfiltered oil complement the raw tuna beautifully. The strongly flavored condiments mixed into the crème fraîche provide just the right amount of contrast and counterpoint to make every morsel of albacore dance in your mouth.

12 ounces sushi-quality albacore tuna,
    cut in ½-inch dice
¼ cup high-quality extra-virgin olive oil,
    such as Spanish Nuñez de Prado
Generous pinch of fleur de sel
2 tablespoons chopped fresh chives
Crème Fraîche and Capers (recipe follows)

Put the tuna in a small mixing bowl and gently toss with enough olive oil to very lightly coat it; season with a generous pinch of fleur de sel. Add the chopped chives and toss gently again to combine.

For a supreme presentation, set a 3-inch ring mold in the center of a small plate and spoon a quarter of the tuna tartare into it to fill; press down gently with the back of a spoon to hold the tuna together. Carefully remove the ring, so the tartare keeps its round shape; repeat with the remaining servings. Alternatively, simply spoon a portion of the tartare on each of the 4 plates. Top the tuna tartare with a small dollop or quenelle of crème fraîche and capers and serve.

crème fraîche and capers

MAKES ½ TO ¾ CUP

2 plum tomatoes, peeled, seeded,
    and finely diced
¼ teaspoon kosher salt
½ cup crème fraîche
2 shallots, minced
6 cornichons, drained and finely chopped
2 tablespoons capers, drained,
    rinsed, and finely chopped
Juice of ½ lemon
Pinch of piment d'Espelette or hot paprika
    (see Ingredient Note)

Put the diced tomatoes in a small bowl, sprinkle them with the salt, and toss. Transfer the tomatoes to a strainer or colander and set over the bowl to drain for 30 minutes; a fair amount of tomato water will leach out. This step is important to keep the water from diluting the crème fraîche and making it runny. Discard the drained water and pat the tomatoes dry with paper towels.

Put the crème fraîche in a large bowl and whisk until it firms up slightly, about 1 minute. Fold in the shallots, cornichons, capers, and tomatoes. Add the lemon juice and piment d'Espelette. Whisk the crème fraîche again lightly to incorporate all the ingredients, but don't overwhip or it can become grainy.

INGREDIENT NOTE: PIMENT D'ESPELETTE

Piment d'Espelette, or the Espelette pepper, is a long, red pepper cultivated in the Basque region of France. It has the same level of heat as hot paprika, in fact, paprika powder can be substituted. The Espelette pepper is regarded as a four on the heat scale of one (mildest) to ten (hottest). Its smoky flavor adds depth to many dishes, rather than intense spiciness. Piment d'Espelette was granted A.O.C. status in 1999, thus helping to ensure that this unique spice will continue to be produced. (A.O.C. stands for Appellation d'Origine Contrôlée. It is a law that guarantees that a product of quality has been made within a specified region following established methods of production.)

HAMACHI WITH SOY-SHERRY REDUCTION SERVES 4

Hamachi is a rich and luxurious fish with a somewhat fatty mouthfeel. The julienned radish and scallion are visually striking against the white stage the fish presents. These garnishes also offer a great textural and flavor contrast to the buttery consistency of the hamachi. The soy-sherry reduction is packed with flavor; the salt from the soy, the acid from the vinegar, the garlic, and citrus zest all play against the richness of the fish.

This simply delicious soy-sherry sauce is great on almost everything and it keeps for weeks in the refrigerator. Brush the sauce on ribs when grilling, marinate chicken with it, serve it with roasted duck or pan-seared salmon; it's also fantastic for dipping spring rolls or dim sum.

1 cup cream sherry, such as Harveys Bristol Cream

1 cup apple cider vinegar

1 cup low-sodium soy sauce

½ cup sugar

2 heads of garlic, unpeeled, coarsely chopped

2 oranges, peeled in strips and juiced (about ⅔ cup)

1 each peeled watermelon radish and unpeeled black radish, or you may substitute one 1-inch piece peeled daikon radish, julienned or shredded (see Ingredient Note)

2 scallions, green parts only, julienned

12 ounces sushi-quality hamachi or yellowtail, or 4 (3-ounce) pieces (see Ingredient Note)

1 teaspoon shichimi togarashi (optional; see Ingredient Note)

½ lime

To make the soy-sherry reduction, in a large saucepan, combine the sherry, vinegar, soy sauce, sugar, garlic, orange peel, and juice. Place over medium heat and stir occasionally to dissolve the sugar. Slowly simmer for 30 to 40 minutes, until the liquid is reduced by two-thirds, to about 1 cup. Strain the sauce into a small bowl and discard the solids. Set aside to completely cool to room temperature or you may refrigerate; the sauce will thicken as it cools.

While the sauce is reducing, fill a large bowl with ice water and put the julienned radishes and scallions in it for about 15 minutes to crisp them up; this step also takes away some of their strong flavor. Put the julienned vegetables in a salad spinner or pat with paper towels to dry well.

Using a very sharp fillet knife, slice the hamachi paper-thin on a slight angle.

To serve, divide the hamachi among 4 chilled plates, shingling the pieces in one thin layer, covering the surface completely. Scatter with a few strands of radish and scallion, drizzle about 1 tablespoon of soy-sherry reduction around each portion. Be very sparing when saucing the plate; a little of the soy-sherry reduction goes a long way. Finish the dish with a very light dusting of shichimi togarashi and squeeze a few drops of fresh lime juice on the hamachi.

INGREDIENT NOTE: WATERMELON AND BLACK RADISHES

Watermelon radish is also known as Roseheart or Shinrimei radish, which in Chinese means "Beauty in the Heart," a name that reflects its gorgeous red flesh. This Asian variety looks like a large pale green turnip, rimmed with a band of white skin that covers a bright magenta inner flesh that resembles watermelon. The round root vegetable is related to the turnip and horseradish family, with a crunchy-crisp texture and a mild to sweet peppery flavor. Black radishes have a pungent flavor and are drier than most other radish varieties. The skin is sooty black on the outside and the flesh within is white. These rather large radishes are grown in the winter.

INGREDIENT NOTE: HAMACHI

The Japanese variety of yellowtail, with mildly sweet flavor and a buttery texture, hamachi is well suited to being eaten raw. Yellowtail is the common name of a number of species of the amberjack family, which are sleek migratory fish similar to tuna.

INGREDIENT NOTE: SHICHIMI TOGARASHI

A peppery Japanese spice mixture made of seven different seasonings, the powder has potent flavor and adds a colorful look to this tuna dish. In the Japanese household, this table condiment is often sprinkled on soups and noodles. The aroma comes from crushed hot chili peppers, peppercorns, dried orange peel, sesame seeds, poppy seeds, and roasted nori. Shichimi togarashi is not that difficult to find these days; it comes in a shaker bottle and can be found in the Asian section of the grocery store or at Asian markets.

ABOVE: HAMACHI WITH SOY-SHERRY REDUCTION. RIGHT: KUMAMOTO OYSTERS WITH CHAMPAGNE MIGNONETTE.

The less oysters are handled, the better; shuck them, serve them, and eat them. It's a good idea to invest in a couple of oyster knives, which are inexpensive and built for the purpose of shucking. Some people use a butter knife or church key as a substitute, but I find those tools break the oyster shells and don't work very well, not to mention that they can be kind of dangerous. As a practice, it is always best to use the right tool for the right job.

At Lever House we serve Kumamoto oysters almost exclusively. I find Kumamotos to have just the right amount of salinity while also offering a certain melonesque or cucumberlike flavor that East Coast oysters generally don't possess. Just be sure to buy oysters from a reliable fishmonger who sells through his supply every few days. It's a good idea to purchase a few more than you plan on serving. One or two might break or you might get a dud, and there isn't anything quite as sad as not having enough oysters.

Mignonette is a classic vinegar-based condiment that complements briny oysters; the addition of effervescent champagne dries out the abrasive tartness of the vinegar. The cocktail sauce is great with poached shrimp, too, and keeps for several weeks in the refrigerator.

**24 fresh Kumamoto oysters, or you
    may substitute Hog Island, Belon,
    Bluepoint, or Malpeque**
Crushed ice
Lemon wedges, for serving
Champagne Mignonette (recipe follows)
Cocktail Sauce (recipe follows)

Scrub the oysters under cold water with a stiff brush to remove the dirt, especially in the hinge area, where mud has a tendency to get trapped. Using a folded dish towel as a mitt, place the oyster, cup side down, in the palm of your towel-covered hand with the hinge facing you. Insert the tip of an oyster knife as far into the hinge as it will go. With gentle force, twist the knife back and forth to pry open the shell. Gently cut the muscle away from the top shell, bend the shell back, and discard it. Run the knife underneath the oyster muscle to detach it completely, but leave it in its shell bed.

Nestle the oysters in a bed of crushed ice to keep them steady. Serve the oysters on the half shell with lemon wedges, champagne mignonette, and cocktail sauce.

champagne mignonette

MAKES ABOUT 1 CUP
$\frac{1}{2}$ cup champagne vinegar
$\frac{1}{2}$ cup dry sparkling wine, such as Spanish
    cava or French champagne
2 shallots, finely diced
3 tablespoons cracked black peppercorns
1 tablespoon caper or cornichon brine

In a small bowl, combine the champagne vinegar, sparkling wine, shallots, black pepper, and brine. Cover and chill for at least 1 hour or up to 1 day before you plan to serve. This allows the flavors to marry and mellow out.

cocktail sauce

MAKES ABOUT 1 CUP
$\frac{1}{2}$ cup ketchup, such as Heinz
$\frac{1}{2}$ cup good-quality barbecue sauce,
    such as Bone Suckin' Sauce
$\frac{1}{4}$ cup grated prepared horseradish, drained
2 tablespoons Worcestershire sauce
3 to 4 drops hot sauce, such as Tabasco

In a mixing bowl whisk together all the ingredients until evenly blended. Chill before serving.

TASMANIAN SEA TROUT GRAVLAX WITH CUCUMBER-CHIVE RELISH SERVES 4

Tasmanian sea trout is from Australia and has the texture and flavor of wild salmon. If your fishmonger can't get Tasmanian sea trout, wild Alaskan salmon or high-quality farmed salmon are more than acceptable substitutes. What I like about this cure is that it is mild yet flavorful and a bit shorter than the traditional three-day gravlax cure (this one takes about a day). The finished product is also slightly more tender (and a little more fragile) than traditional gravlax. If you can find them, black onion seeds (Nigella or Kalonji) look great sprinkled on the orange-red flesh of the gravlax and offer up a crunchy oniony bite that adds texture to the sea trout and cucumber relish. The sea trout gravlax is also fantastic slivered on a bagel with cream cheese or on potato blinis (page 174). Easy to make and wonderfully fresh tasting, the cucumber-chive relish is good in the summer on a grilled piece of fish; the cucumbers cool the onion bite of the chives.

- 1/3 cup kosher salt
- 1/3 cup sugar
- 1/4 teaspoon juniper berries, crushed
- 1/4 teaspoon whole allspice, crushed
- 1/2 teaspoon whole black peppercorns, crushed
- 4 fresh chervil or flat-leaf parsley sprigs, coarsely chopped, plus additional for garnish
- 4 fresh tarragon sprigs, coarsely chopped
- 2 shallots, thickly sliced
- 1 pound Tasmanian sea trout or salmon fillet, skin on, pin bones removed, rinsed under cool water, and patted dry
- Black onion seeds, for garnish (optional; see Ingredient Note)
- Cucumber-Chive Relish (recipe follows)
- Fresh lemon juice, for serving

In a large bowl, combine the salt, sugar, juniper berries, allspice, peppercorns, chervil, tarragon, and shallots; mix well. Sprinkle approximately a quarter of the cure mixture on a glass baking dish and lay the trout in it, skin side down. Pack the remaining cure evenly on top of and around the fish to cover completely.

Wrap the entire dish tightly with a large piece of plastic wrap. Place another baking dish on top of the trout and put something heavy on top to weigh it down, such as a skillet or a half gallon of milk, to press out the moisture from the fish. Refrigerate for 24 to 36 hours to cure, basting once or twice with the liquid that renders from the fish.

Remove the trout from the refrigerator and unwrap carefully. Scrape off the salt mixture and lightly rinse the fish under cool water; pat dry with paper towels. The cured trout will be firm but pliable. Using a very sharp fillet knife, slice the gravlax paper-thin on a slight angle, avoiding the gray fat close to the skin.

To serve, arrange the sliced trout shingled in the center of a platter or individual plates. Sprinkle the gravlax with black onion seeds, if using; spoon a small ribbon of cucumber-chive relish down the middle, garnish the plate with chervil, and squeeze a little bit of lemon juice on the fish. Wrap any leftover cured trout tightly in plastic and hold in the refrigerator for up to a week.

cucumber-chive relish

MAKES ABOUT 1 CUP

1 English cucumber, peeled, seeded, and finely diced
½ teaspoon finely grated lemon zest
¼ cup chopped fresh chives
2 tablespoons extra-virgin olive oil
1 tablespoon fresh lime juice
Freshly ground black pepper

In a large bowl, combine the relish ingredients and mix well with a wooden spoon. Cover and chill for 30 minutes to allow the flavors to marry and mellow.

INGREDIENT NOTE: BLACK ONION SEEDS
Also called Nigella or Kalonji, black onion seeds resemble poppy seeds but have a peppery bite. These small seeds are most often found in Indian cooking and used in breads, such as naan. Black onion seeds are available in Indian and Middle Eastern grocery stores; their inclusion in the gravlax is tasty but not imperative.

TUNA CARPACCIO WITH WASABI CRÈME FRAÎCHE SERVES 4

This light starter is a popular choice at Lever House. If tuna is truly fresh, there are few better ways of serving it than this. The fatty fish holds up to the bold flavors of the sauce and retains a naturally meaty texture.

Several species of tuna are available in the modern market. Bluefin is the most expensive and generally considered the best to serve raw, while yellowfin is a more affordable alternative. For the simple "wow" of the dish, the color of the tuna itself is as important as the overall quality and freshness. Look for bright red flesh, which acts as the palette to show off the vibrant contrast of the green wasabi and shiso. If you can't get really fresh, sushi-quality tuna from your fish market, think of another dish to serve and wait until premium tuna becomes available. Also, when making the wasabi crème fraîche, please follow the recipe to a T.

I must have gone through fifteen different versions of this sauce before hitting on this exact balance of ginger, wasabi paste, lime juice, and crème fraîche. This precise blend offers just the right kick, punch, and zing. If you can't find shiso leaves in an Asian market, just drizzle the tuna with fruity olive oil.

12 ounces sushi-quality tuna, such as yellowfin, thinly sliced, or 4 (3-ounce) pieces
Wasabi Crème Fraîche (recipe follows)
Shiso Oil (recipe follows)
¼ cup wasabi tobiko (flying fish roe), for garnish (optional)

Lay a large sheet of plastic wrap on a countertop. Place the tuna on the plastic wrap and cover with another large piece of plastic on top. Evenly pound the tuna gently between the plastic with a flat mallet or small skillet, until very thin. Keep covered and chilled until serving; the tuna may be prepared a few hours ahead.

To serve, cut the plastic-wrapped tuna in 4 even disks using an inverted bowl or a ring mold as a guide. Peel off the top layer of plastic from the tuna. Invert the carpaccio onto 4 chilled plates, covering the surface completely. Remove the remaining sheets of plastic wrap.

Squeeze decorative stripes of the wasabi crème fraîche across the tuna and drizzle a little shiso oil around the plate. Garnish with a tablespoon of wasabi tobiko on each, if desired.

wasabi crème fraîche

MAKES ABOUT 1¼ CUPS

1⅔ tablespoons freshly grated ginger

1⅔ tablespoons wasabi paste

2 tablespoons fresh lime juice

2 teaspoons kosher salt

1 cup crème fraîche

In a small mixing bowl, blend together the ginger, wasabi, lime juice, and salt until combined well without any lumps. In a separate large bowl, whip the crème fraîche with a wire whisk until it thickens slightly, about 1 minute. Fold the wasabi mixture into the crème fraîche and incorporate evenly. Spoon the wasabi crème fraîche into a plastic squeeze bottle for serving.

shiso oil

MAKES ABOUT ¾ CUP

½ cup packed fresh shiso leaves

¾ cup grapeseed oil

Combine the shiso leaves and oil in a blender and puree for about 5 minutes, until the oil actually gets hot from the agitation of the blades. It should also look very green. Pour the oil though a sieve lined with cheesecloth to filter out the solids and create a clear green oil; put it in a small container and reserve chilled.

Venison has a fine texture, and a flavor similar to beef, but it is generally a much leaner meat. You may substitute beef filet if you'd prefer. The venison loin is pan-seared until the meat is rare, so it is not actually served raw; the term *carpaccio* refers to the preparation of paper-thin slices of chilled meat. The genesis of this carpaccio isn't very glamorous, I'm afraid. After a private event, we had some seared venison left that we put in the freezer. The pickled onions are always on hand because we serve them at lunch with our burger. From there it was only a hop, skip, and a jump to this dish.

Finely chopped pickled onions bring the venison to life. The celery leaves and parsley add a nice herbal note, the mustard seeds a bit of crunch and savory heat.

Avoid the temptation of making the compote in a food processor; the blades of the machine aerate the mixture, making it a paler, less vibrant version of the hand-chopped version. Even without the compote, the pickled red onions are great to have on hand as a multipurpose condiment; try them on sandwiches or burgers and let your imagination go from there. The pickled onions keep for weeks in an airtight container in the refrigerator and the recipe can easily be doubled, so it makes sense to prepare a bigger batch. You may also use this pickling method on just about any vegetable, such as bell peppers, zucchini, and cauliflower.

¼ cup Spice Mix (page 228)
1 extremely fresh venison loin (about
    1 pound), trimmed of all fat and sinew
Kosher salt
2 tablespoons canola oil
½ cup Pickled Red Onion Compote
    (recipe follows)
Generous pinch of fleur de sel
¼ cup finely chopped fresh chives,
    for garnish
¼ cup peppery sprouts, such as watercress
    or mustard sprouts, for garnish

Spread the spice mix on a flat plate. Season the venison all around with a generous sprinkling of kosher salt, and roll the loin in the fragrant spice mix to lightly coat.

Place a large cast-iron skillet over medium heat. Coat the bottom of the pan with the oil and when it gets hazy, carefully add the venison loin and sear on all sides, about 3 minutes total time. The meat inside should still be rare. Remove the venison from the heat and cool completely.

Wrap the venison tightly in plastic wrap and set in the freezer to firm up and chill for 30 minutes. This will make it easier to slice thinly. Make sure the venison is very cold, and then cut it into the thinnest possible slices, using a razor-sharp, thin-bladed knife.

To serve, divide the thinly sliced venison among 4 chilled plates, arranging the slices in a rosette pattern, with a piece of venison in the center and shingled slices in a circle around it. Put about 2 tablespoons of the pickled red onion compote on the center of the carpaccio; at the restaurant we use a pastry bag to pipe it out decoratively, but a tablespoon will work, too. Season the venison carpaccio lightly with fleur de sel; scatter the chopped chives and sprouts on top to garnish.

pickled red onions

MAKES ABOUT 2 CUPS

3 cups distilled white vinegar

1 1/2 cups sugar

1 cinnamon stick, broken in half

1 whole star anise

1 whole clove

1/8 teaspoon whole allspice

1/2 teaspoon whole black peppercorns

1 dried chili

2 bay leaves

2 firm red onions (about 1 pound), sliced into
  1/4-inch-thick rounds and separated into
  individual rings

To make the pickling brine, combine the vinegar, sugar, cinnamon stick, star anise, clove, allspice, peppercorns, chili, and bay leaves in a large saucepan. Slowly bring to a boil over medium heat, stirring occasionally to dissolve the sugar. Reduce the heat to low, cover, and gently simmer for 3 minutes, until the mixture is fragrant and the sugar is completely dissolved. Turn off the heat and let the mixture sit to infuse more flavor into the brine.

After it has rested and cooled off a bit, pour the brine through a strainer into another pot to remove the solids, place the strained brine over medium heat, and bring to a boil again. Working in batches, add a few handfuls of the onions to the brine and blanch for only about 30 seconds. Carefully scoop out the onions with a slotted spoon and put them on a side plate to cool. Continue this process until all the onions are blanched in the brine.

Repeat the cycle 2 more times, so all the onions have been blanched in the brine 3 times total, always cooling the onions between blanches; this technique sets the red color of the onions and cooks them while leaving them crunchy. After the last round of blanching, cool the brine and the onions separately. Put the onions in a container, pour the brine over them to cover, and chill. The pickled red onions keep for weeks stored in the refrigerator.

pickled red onion compote

MAKES 1/2 CUP

1 tablespoon whole yellow mustard seeds

1/4 cup dry white wine, such as Sauvignon Blanc

1/2 cup drained Pickled Red Onions (recipe
  above), finely chopped

2 tablespoons finely chopped fresh
  flat-leaf parsley

2 tablespoons finely chopped celery leaves

1 tablespoon extra-virgin olive oil

Kosher salt and freshly ground black pepper

Pinch of Aleppo pepper (see Ingredient Note)
  or cayenne

In a small saucepan over medium heat, combine the mustard seeds and wine and bring to a boil. Turn off the flame and let the mustard seeds steep in the hot wine for 10 minutes to mellow and soften. Drain the wine and put the mustard seeds in a small bowl. Add the chopped pickled onions, parsley, celery leaves, and oil. Season to taste with salt and pepper, and add the Aleppo; mix until well combined.

INGREDIENT NOTE: ALEPPO PEPPER

Aleppo pepper is one of the most versatile spices in the Lever House kitchen; once you start using it, you wonder how you ever lived without it. You will taste it often in our recipes. With its high oil content, dried crushed Aleppo pepper has moderate heat that doesn't overpower its fruity flavor. The dark red and robust chili pepper is so named for the Aleppo region of Syria.

When most people hear "salsa verde," they imagine a spicy tomatillo salsa created in Mexico. Italian salsa verde is a pungent parsley sauce that is more similar to a green pesto. Arugula gives this variation a peppery kick that's a nice match for meats. As an alternative to carpaccio, grill the beef tenderloin and serve with the salsa and capers or pickled red onions (page 49). The crisp fried capers are also good to have around to toss in salads or pasta; they're even addictive just for snacking.

12 ounces extremely fresh beef tenderloin, trimmed of all fat and sinew
Arugula Salsa Verde (recipe follows)
1 (2-ounce) wedge Parmigiano-Reggiano
Crispy Capers (recipe follows)
3 tablespoons chopped fresh chives
Generous pinch of fleur de sel

Wrap the beef tightly in plastic and place in the freezer for approximately 30 minutes to firm up and make it easier to slice paper-thin.

Unwrap the beef and, using a very sharp knife, slice it as thinly as possible. Divide the beef among 4 chilled plates, shingling them in one thin layer, covering the surface completely. Squeeze decorative stripes of the salsa verde across the beef. Using a vegetable peeler, shave curls of Parmigiano from the wedge of cheese and scatter on the beef carpaccio. Top each serving with a tablespoon of the crispy capers, a shower of chopped chives, and a sprinkle of fleur de sel; serve at once.

arugula salsa verde

MAKES ABOUT ½ CUP

¼ cup arugula, rinsed, dried, and coarsely chopped
2 tablespoons capers, drained, rinsed, and coarsely chopped
½ jalapeño, seeded and coarsely chopped
½ shallot, coarsely chopped
2 anchovy fillets, coarsely chopped
1 teaspoon finely grated lemon zest
1 tablespoon freshly squeezed lemon juice, plus more if needed
½ cup extra-virgin olive oil
Kosher salt and freshly ground black pepper, if needed

Combine the arugula, capers, jalapeño, shallot, anchovies, lemon zest, and juice in a blender. Pulse on and off until the mixture is finely chopped. With the motor running, slowly pour in the oil in a steady stream to produce a bright green puree. Taste and check for seasoning, add salt, pepper, or more lemon juice to balance out the flavor. Spoon the salsa verde into a plastic squeeze bottle for serving.

crispy capers

MAKES ½ CUP

½ cup capers, drained and dried well
Vegetable oil, for frying

Heat approximately ¼ inch of oil in a small sauté pan until very hot but not smoking. Very carefully add the capers to the hot oil (they will spit and bubble). Gently stir once and when the capers become crisp, after about 30 to 45 seconds, remove them with a slotted spoon to a plate lined with paper towels. The crispy capers may be made in advance and kept in a tightly covered container at room temperature until needed.

Someone I worked for years ago once told me that diners remember particularly the first and last things they eat at a restaurant. I believe it. That is why it is especially important that a restaurant's appetizers (and desserts) fire on all cylinders. Appetizers should draw you in, sate your hunger a bit, tantalize and perk up your taste buds, and make you excited about the entrées and desserts to come. Whether it's a composed salad, a hot meat or fish item, or raw fish or shellfish, the ingredients must be of the highest quality and freshness.

Salads should be lightly dressed with vinaigrette, and meat or fish judiciously sauced. Make sure that the main ingredients are well seasoned and that the vinaigrette or sauce is seasoned as well. Many a dish comes up a little short because of an underseasoned sauce. If you have a doubt about the seasoning of a sauce or vinaigrette, taste a little of it on a leaf of lettuce or piece of the protein you are serving. This simple test is a good gauge of seasoning levels.

APPETIZERS

What might at first appear to be a well-seasoned, balanced vinaigrette, when tasted on a salad

ingredient, might reveal the need for more salt, vinegar, etc. The lesson: taste, taste, and taste again.

One thing I've learned about myself over the years is that I love to adjust flavors into the higher

registers. The flavors of citrus (grapefruit, lemons, limes, and oranges) as well as the winy tang that

good vinegar can add to a salad or sauce help to focus and concentrate flavor when used sensibly.

Now that I have made you aware of my passion for well-seasoned food with good acidity, the

only thing left for me to tell you is to enjoy the recipes!

PINK GRAPEFRUIT, AVOCADO, AND BOTTARGA SALAD <small>SERVES 4</small>

Even though bottarga (the sun-dried roe of gray mullet) is a slightly unusual ingredient, this is a very popular salad at Lever House. Grapefruit and avocado is a classic combo; the addition of shaved bottarga is both a colorful and flavorful enhancement. This composed salad requires a bit of preparation, but once you have all the ingredients ready, it is quick to assemble. Like all vinaigrettes in this book, the champagne-grapefruit vinaigrette may be prepared a day in advance and refrigerated.

1 fennel bulb, trimmed, halved, and
  very thinly sliced
2 ruby red grapefruits, seedless
1½ ripe Hass avocados, halved, pitted,
  peeled, and largely diced
Juice of 1 lime
2 celery stalks, peeled and finely sliced
  on the bias
2 scallions, green parts only, sliced
  on the bias
¼ cup baby arugula, rinsed and dried
3 to 4 tablespoons Champagne-Grapefruit
  Vinaigrette (recipe follows)
Kosher salt and freshly ground black pepper
Shaved or grated bottarga (see
  Ingredient Note)

Fill a medium mixing bowl with ice water and soak the fennel slices for about 15 minutes to crisp them up. Put the fennel in a salad spinner or pat with paper towels to dry well.

To segment the grapefruit, first trim the top and bottom flat so it stands steady on a work surface; cut deep enough so you see the meat of the fruit. Using a paring knife, cut off the skin and bitter white pith of the fruit, following the natural round shape and turning the grapefruit as you do so. Trim off any white areas that remain. Hold the grapefruit over a bowl to catch the juices. Carefully cut along the mem-brane, on both sides of each segment, to free the pieces, and let them drop into the bowl. Then squeeze the membrane over the wedges in the bowl to extract the remaining juice. Reserve 1 tablespoon of the juice for use in the vinaigrette.

Lightly toss the diced avocado with the lime juice to prevent browning; make sure the pieces are coated evenly and the avocado doesn't smash like guacamole.

In a mixing bowl, combine the fennel slices, avocado, celery, scallions, and arugula. Dress the salad with 3 to 4 tablespoons of the champagne-grapefruit vinaigrette and gently toss using your hands to combine; season with salt and pepper.

To serve, arrange the grapefruit segments in star patterns on 4 plates, put a pile of the salad on top of each, and finish off with a nice amount of the shaved bottarga.

INGREDIENT NOTE: BOTTARGA

A specialty of the islands of Sardinia and Sicily, bottarga is often called the Italian caviar. This Mediterranean delicacy is made from the salted, pressed, and sun-dried roe of either tuna (*bottarga di tonno*) or mullet (*bottarga di muggine*); the latter is a bit milder and more subtle than the tuna variety, which can be quite strong and sharp. Sardinians commonly serve bottarga simply shaved over pasta with garlic, parsley, and extra-virgin olive oil. The dried and salted roe is sold vacuum-packed and looks like red sticks, almost like a tongue! Bottarga can be a little expensive, but is well worth its distinctive flavor. If you can't find bottarga online or in an Italian market, there really is no substitute. Although still tasty without it, this salad is truly out of this world with shaved bottarga on top. A little goes a long way, but if you got it . . . use it.

champagne-grapefruit vinaigrette

MAKES ABOUT ¾ CUP

1 tablespoon fresh grapefruit juice, reserved
  from salad
1 tablespoon champagne vinegar
½ tablespoon minced scallion, white part only
Pinch of Aleppo pepper (see Ingredient Note,
  page 49) or cayenne
½ cup extra-virgin olive oil
Kosher salt and freshly ground black pepper

In a mixing bowl, combine the grapefruit juice, vinegar, scallion, and Aleppo pepper. Slowly add the oil in a stream while whisking to emulsify the vinaigrette; season with salt and pepper. Keep any leftover vinaigrette covered in the refrigerator for up to 3 days.

Nage literally means "swim" in French. In the French kitchen, nage is an aromatic broth typically used to gently poach seafood; the most notable of these classic dishes is *lobster à la nage*. We use scallops at the restaurant for their meaty sweetness. Nage is not really a soup; it's more a fragrant bouillon that serves to moisten the seafood, not drown it. All flavors in a nage have to be balanced; no ingredient should overpower the others . . . in other words, it's culinary alchemy. The acidity of the vinegar and white wine, mixed with the sweet vegetables, and the kick from the spices, produce an unassuming clear liquid with surprising depth of flavor; it's all packed in there. The nage takes a little time to make, but it's primarily gently simmering on the stove without a lot of fuss. Any leftover makes a great base for soup.

A diver scallop is exactly what the name means—scallops that are collected from the ocean by divers hand-picking each one. Diver scallops tend to be fresher than other types. Always choose dry scallops, which have not been plumped up with water or chemicals like scallops labeled *wet*.

1½ cups Nage (recipe follows)
8 large diver scallops (about 1 pound)
Pinch of kosher salt
Pinch of Aleppo pepper (see Ingredient Note, page 49) or cayenne
2 tablespoons extra-virgin olive oil
4 red radishes, julienned
2 tablespoons chopped fresh chives, for garnish
2 tablespoons chopped fresh chervil or flat-leaf parsley, for garnish

Prepare the nage and keep warm.

Place a nonstick pan over medium-high heat. Season the scallops with kosher salt and Aleppo pepper. Drizzle about 2 tablespoons of olive oil into the pan and when it just gets hazy, add the scallops. Sear the scallops for 1 to 2 minutes, without moving them around; just let them do their thing. When the underside of the scallops looks caramelized, turn them over and sear the other side for another 30 seconds. Put the scallops on a side plate lined with paper towels to blot some of the oil. Take note that the scallops will still be rare; they'll continue to cook in the hot nage.

To serve, heat 4 small soup bowls. Divide the radish julienne among the bowls, ladle a little more than ¼ cup of nage over each serving, and set 2 scallops per person on the radishes. Garnish with a sprinkle of chives and chervil.

nage

MAKES ABOUT 2 QUARTS

½ onion, halved
½ tomato, cored
½ fennel bulb, halved
1 celery stalk, halved
¼ carrot, halved
2 garlic cloves
1½ teaspoons whole white peppercorns
1½ teaspoons whole Szechwan peppercorns
1½ teaspoons fennel seeds
1½ teaspoons cardamom pods
1½ teaspoons sea salt
1 bay leaf
¼ cup white wine vinegar
1 cup dry white wine, such as Sauvignon Blanc
2 quarts water

To make the nage, put all the ingredients in a large soup pot. Bring slowly up to a boil over medium-low heat; the goal is to gently extract as much flavor as possible out of the vegetables and spices and into the liquid. Reduce to low and simmer slowly, uncovered, for 3½ hours; "low and slow" is the mantra, there should not be a lot of evaporation. Skim any impurities that rise to the surface during cooking.

Turn off the heat and let the nage steep for 10 minutes and cool a bit. Slowly pour the broth through a strainer into another pot to remove the solids; don't press down on the ingredients. The broth should be clear, not cloudy. Cover, and keep warm while preparing the scallops.

This is a version of the renowned French classic *Magret de Canard aux Cerises*, duck with sour cherry sauce. The unctuous duck and tart cherries play off each other in harmony. The ease of this recipe, along with the fact that it is impressive and delicious, makes this a real winner. In season, please search out and use fresh sour cherries; if they aren't available, fresh bing cherries are also nice. If saba, or vin cotto, isn't available, don't hesitate to substitute a good balsamic vinegar.

This simple appetizer will also make a wonderful main course. Just increase the serving size of the duck breast and consider serving with Potato Gratin (page 175) and Haricots Verts (page 169).

½ cup pitted sour cherries, fresh or frozen and thawed

1 cup saba/vin cotto (see Ingredient Note) or balsamic vinegar

Several turns of freshly ground black pepper, plus additional to taste

2 boneless duck breast halves (about 8 ounces each), skin on and excess fat trimmed

Kosher salt

Fresh chervil or flat-leaf parsley, for garnish

Put the cherries in a saucepan and pour in the saba to cover. Simmer gently over medium-low heat for 30 minutes, until syrupy. Grind lots of black pepper into the cherries to balance out the sweetness. Cover and keep the cherry sauce warm.

Using a sharp knife, score the skin of the duck by slicing lines across the breasts and then cut diagonally down the slashes to make a diamond pattern; take care not to cut too deeply and pierce the flesh. Season the duck breasts generously with salt and pepper.

Place a dry sauté or grill pan over medium heat. When it's hot, add the duck breasts, skin side down; duck is notoriously fatty, so no need to add oil to the pan. Sear the breasts until the skin is crispy and the fat is rendered, about 10 to 12 minutes. Tip out the excess fat that collects in the pan a couple of times, so the duck breasts sear, not fry. (The reserved duck fat is a delicacy and great to have on hand; use it to sauté potatoes and onions.) Turn over the duck breasts and cook another 2 to 3 minutes, for medium-rare. Remove the duck to a side plate or wire rack for 5 minutes to rest. Using a very sharp knife, cut the duck breasts into ¼-inch-thick slices on a slight angle.

To serve, fan the slices of duck among 4 plates, skin side up. Put 2 generous tablespoons of the sour cherries at the top of each duck breast fan, drizzle some of the saba juice over the meat, and garnish with chervil.

INGREDIENT NOTE: SABA/VIN COTTO

Those familiar with Italian cuisine will recognize the ingredient saba, the sweet reduction of grape must, or cooked grape juice. Saba is produced by slowly simmering the must from the trebbiano grape, the same used for balsamic vinegar, except cooked down even more, until it turns sweet and syrupy. With a wonderful fruity character, saba has notes of ripe grapes, sweet plums, and raisins. It's a nice item to have in your pantry. Try drizzling it over cheesecake, dressing a fruit salad, using it in marinades, or splashing a little over ice cream. In the south of Italy, saba is called vin cotto. It can be found at Italian specialty markets and some grocery stores.

FARM GREENS WITH RICOTTA SALATA, BUTTERNUT SQUASH, AND HAZELNUTS SERVES 4

Everyone who tries this salad falls in love with it. Crisp greens, roasted butternut squash, toasted hazelnuts, slightly salty and tangy ricotta salata—all are brought together and lightly tossed with a fruity vinaigrette. The combination of deep sweetness and slightly mouth-puckering acidity in the pomegranate molasses works incredibly well to bring out the best of all the ingredients in the salad. By all means, search out this thick, dark syrup not only to make this dressing, but to welcome it as a pantry staple. You could substitute pomegranate molasses in just about any recipe that calls for balsamic vinegar, too. The sweetly tart pomegranate vinaigrette keeps for three or four days covered in the refrigerator.

1 large butternut squash (about 2 pounds)
2 tablespoons grapeseed oil
Kosher salt and freshly ground black pepper
¼ cup blanched hazelnuts
1 to 1½ cups baby greens (any good, local crisp lettuces), washed and spun dry
1 cup coarsely grated ricotta salata
¼ cup Pomegranate Vinaigrette (recipe follows)

Preheat the oven to 375°F.

The butternut squash is vaguely pear shaped, wide at the bottom and skinnier at the top. For this recipe, we use only the narrow necks of the squash; the skin tends to be softer and there aren't any seeds and stringy membranes to deal with. (Save the big part of the squash for another use.) Using a heavy chef's knife or a cleaver, cut off the squash's neck, right about where the bulbous bottom meets it. With a vegetable peeler or paring knife, peel off the skin to expose the orange flesh. Cut the squash into ½-inch cubes and put them in a medium mixing bowl. There should be about 1 cup.

Toss the squash cubes with the oil to coat well; season with salt and pepper. Spread the squash on a foil-lined sheet pan and roast for 10 to 12 minutes, rotating the pan halfway through baking so it cooks evenly. The butternut squash should look caramelized and golden on the surface and just be tender when pierced with a knife. As an alternative, sauté the cubes of squash in grapeseed oil in a large pan over medium heat, for about 8 minutes, until cooked through and golden. Put the roasted squash on a side plate to cool.

While the squash is cooling, spread the hazelnuts on a small pan and bake in the oven to toast lightly for 5 to 7 minutes. Let the nuts cool, and then break them down the middle, at the natural seam. Use your fingers or the flat side of a knife to split them in half.

In a large bowl, combine the lettuces, butternut squash, hazelnuts, and half of the ricotta salata; season well with pepper and lightly with salt (the cheese can be quite salty). Dress the salad with the pomegranate vinaigrette, about ¼ cup (salads are best well dressed, where each leaf is filmed with the vinaigrette, *not drenched*). Toss the ingredients gently using your hands to combine.

To serve, divide the salad among 4 plates, trying to equally distribute the lettuce and the goodies for each portion. Sprinkle the rest of the cheese on top of the salads and finish off with a final grinding of black pepper.

pomegranate vinaigrette

MAKES ABOUT 1½ CUPS

2 large shallots, finely diced

Pinch of kosher salt

2 tablespoons pomegranate molasses

2 tablespoons red wine vinegar

1 cup grapeseed oil

Freshly ground black pepper

Put the diced shallots in a mixing bowl and sprinkle with a healthy pinch of salt. Let them sit for 5 minutes to allow the salt to draw out the water from the shallots, which will ultimately help hold together the vinaigrette. Add the pomegranate molasses and the vinegar and whisk with the shallots to combine. Slowly add the oil in a stream while whisking to emulsify the vinaigrette, until the dressing thickens and comes together. Add a few twists of black pepper to balance it out. Keep any leftover vinaigrette covered in the refrigerator for up to 3 days.

GRILLED SHORT RIBS WITH FRISÉE SERVES 4

What is slightly unusual and great about this preparation is the relatively short cooking time. Beef short ribs are commonly braised for hours. These ribs are grilled from raw to medium-rare, a process that doesn't take much more than 15 minutes. Sliced thinly across the grain, the dense marbling of the muscle in the short ribs makes for a surprisingly tender taste. The rich, beefy flavor of the ribs is offset by the slight bitterness of the frisée and the sharp intensity of the anchovy vinaigrette. The Caesar-inspired anchovy vinaigrette will keep covered in the refrigerator for three or four days and is ideal to drizzle on romaine hearts. This meat-lovers salad makes a satisfying and elegant first course or light lunch.

¼ cup Spice Mix (page 228)
4 boneless beef short ribs (4 ounces each)
Kosher salt
2 tablespoons vegetable oil
½ to ¾ cup frisée, curly endive, or chicory lettuce, washed and dried
Freshly ground black pepper
3 to 4 tablespoons Anchovy Vinaigrette/ Caesar Dressing (recipe follows)
2 tablespoons chopped fresh chives

Spread the spice mix on a flat plate. Season the beef ribs all around with salt, and dredge them in the fragrant spice mix to lightly coat. Drizzle both sides of the ribs with the oil.

Heat a grill pan or cast-iron skillet over medium flame; don't turn it up too high and have it screaming hot or the outside of the beef will burn before the inside is cooked. Grill the short ribs for about 3 minutes per side, turning with tongs; for all 4 sides, this takes about 12 minutes total time. The meat should still be medium-rare. Remove the beef ribs to a cutting board, cover to keep warm, and let rest for 5 minutes to allow the juices to settle.

While the meat is resting, put the frisée in a mixing bowl and season with salt and pepper. Drizzle with 3 to 4 tablespoons of the anchovy vinaigrette, tossing with your hands to dress the salad lightly and evenly.

Using a sharp knife, cut the beef short ribs against the grain on a slight angle into very thin slices; slicing against the grain ensures that the meat doesn't taste tough and stringy.

To serve, divide the beef among 4 plates, fanning the slices in a semicircle. Put a small pile of the dressed frisée in the bay created by the fanned meat. Drizzle the beef with a little anchovy vinaigrette and shower with chopped chives.

anchovy vinaigrette/caesar dressing
MAKES ABOUT 2 CUPS
10 anchovy fillets, packed in oil
2 garlic cloves
1 large egg yolk
1 tablespoon red wine vinegar
Juice of 1 lemon
1½ cups extra-virgin olive oil
¼ cup coarsely grated Parmigiano-Reggiano
Pinch of freshly ground black pepper

To make the vinaigrette, put the anchovies and garlic in a blender and puree well. While the motor is still running, drop in the yolk and incorporate. Add the vinegar and lemon juice and continue to blend. Slowly drizzle in the olive oil until the dressing thickens. Stop the blender, add the cheese, and quickly blend again for 5 seconds to mix; the Parmesan should still have a slightly chunky texture. Add a pinch of pepper to balance out the salt of the anchovies and cheese. Cover and chill for at least 1 hour. Before using, mix it again with a whisk to bring the dressing back together. As an alternative, this dressing can be made by hand in a large mortar and pestle . . . with some elbow grease.

Seared foie gras is so ubiquitous on restaurant menus these days. At Lever House, we offer a slight twist on pan-seared foie gras; we grill the liver instead and serve it with a seasonal fruit garnish. Winter is the season for citrus, so we often pair the foie with juicy blood oranges; spring brings rhubarb; summer months bear apricots, peaches, and nectarines; and fall gives us the gift of quince—one of the most underrated and underutilized fruits I know of. The quintessential quince is an aromatic fruit that looks like a cross between a golden apple and a large lumpy lemon. Although quince has a beguiling fragrance, raw quince is mouth puckering in the extreme. When poached or roasted, quince mellows to a sweet pineapplelike taste with a hint of tartness that truly blossoms. The brilliant golden pink syrup quince exudes when roasted works wonderfully with the foie gras. Make the quince puree a day or two in advance and keep any leftovers. For a Latin American flair, spread quince puree on bread and serve with shaved Manchego or Cabrales cheese.

1 (¾- to 1-pound) Grade A lobe duck foie
 gras, chilled
Kosher salt and freshly ground black pepper
Quince Puree (recipe follows)
Spiced Walnuts (recipe follows)

Rinse the foie gras and remove the veins and tough membranes. Using a sharp knife dipped in hot water, cut the foie gras on a slight bias into 3- to 4-ounce medallions, approximately 1 inch thick; you should have at least 4 pieces. Season the medallions on both sides generously with salt and pepper.

Place a grill pan or cast-iron skillet over medium-high heat, no need to coat with oil. When the pan is nice and hot, add the foie gras pieces and sear for 2 minutes, until caramelized. Carefully tip out a bit of the rendered duck fat into a disposable container. Using a spatula, turn over the foie and cook for another minute or two. Remove to a warmed platter lined with paper towels to drain.

To serve, put a foie gras medallion in the center of each of 4 plates, spoon a nice-sized dollop of the quince puree to rest on the edge of the foie. Garnish with the spiced walnuts and sprinkle with a little salt. Serve warm and enjoy the rich decadence.

quince puree

MAKES ABOUT 2 CUPS

4 large quinces (about 3 pounds), washed,
 dried, and halved lengthwise
2¼ teaspoons kosher salt
1 cup sugar
1 orange, halved

Preheat the oven to 350°F.

Rub the salt into the cut sides of the quince to draw out the juices and balance out their sweetness. Pour the sugar into a small sheet pan with a lip or a glass baking dish, and spread it evenly to cover the bottom. Put the quince halves, cut side down, in the sugar. Squeeze half of the orange over the quinces, extracting as much juice as possible. Cut the remaining orange half into ¼-inch-thick slices and wedge the pieces between the quince halves; the flavor will penetrate the quince. Bake for 1 hour, until the quinces are soft and easily pierced with a knife and the sugar melts and it all bubbles together into a syrup.

Once the quinces are cool enough to handle, peel the skins off with a knife and scoop out the seeds and cores; discard the orange slices. Put the quince flesh and the rendered pink jelly in a food processor; puree until smooth. Reserve warm. The quince puree can be made several days in advance; cool it before storing it covered in the refrigerator, and simply heat before serving.

spiced walnuts

MAKES 1 CUP

1 cup walnut pieces
1 teaspoon ground cinnamon
¼ teaspoon salt
Generous pinch of freshly ground black pepper
Pinch of cayenne
¼ cup dark brown sugar, lightly packed
2 tablespoons melted unsalted butter
1 tablespoon water

Preheat the oven to 350°F. For ease, the nuts can be made while baking the quinces.

To make the spiced walnuts, combine all ingredients in a mixing bowl and toss to coat the nuts in the mixture. Line a sheet pan with a Silpat or parchment paper and spread the nuts in an even layer on the pan. Bake the nuts for 5 to 8 minutes, until dry, toasty, and tasty. Check the nuts after 5 minutes to be sure they don't burn; if they do, start over. Cool the spiced walnuts to room temperature. They will keep for a few days, tightly covered and stored in a dry place. The nuts are also really good just for noshing!

GRILLED SHRIMP WITH CHERRY TOMATOES, ROSEMARY, AND CHICKPEA PUREE SERVES 4

Years ago while traveling in southern Italy, I had a dish of really fresh shrimp, grilled over a wood fire, served with chickpeas dressed very simply with good extra-virgin olive oil. Those flavors have stayed with me. I've chosen to turn the chickpeas (and a little extra-virgin olive oil) into a puree, marinate the shrimp to give them a little bit more punch, and add cherry tomatoes as little exclamation points of flavor. Please use fresh herbs for this preparation; their essential oils impart an herbaceous nuance to the dish. If you are landlocked, frozen shrimp work very well in this recipe. We use Maya in the restaurant, but any quality frozen and thawed product will suffice. The dried chickpeas need to soak in water for a day, so plan accordingly. Leftover chickpea puree can be served as an impromptu hummus dip with pita wedges and cut vegetables. The whole cooked chickpeas can also be tossed in salads.

4 garlic cloves, smashed

2 fresh bay leaves, bruised and halved

1 Meyer or sweet lemon, quartered and sliced ¼ inch thick

Pinch of Aleppo pepper (see Ingredient Note, page 49) or cayenne

¼ cup extra-virgin olive oil, plus 2 tablespoons

12 large shrimp (about 1 to 1½ pounds), peeled and deveined with heads and tails on preferred

Sea salt and freshly ground black pepper

10 cherry tomatoes, halved

1 cup Chickpea Puree (recipe follows)

1 tablespoon chopped fresh chives, for garnish

To make a quick marinade for the shrimp, combine the garlic, bay leaves, lemon slices, Aleppo pepper, and ¼ cup olive oil in a large bowl. Add the shrimp, tossing to coat. Allow to marinate for 1 hour in the refrigerator.

Scrape off the marinade solids and season the shrimp with a generous amount of salt and pepper. Heat a grill pan or cast-iron skillet over medium flame. Grill the shrimp for 3 minutes, then turn them over with tongs and cook for another 2 minutes, about 5 minutes total. The shrimp should feel firm and the flesh look opaque. Give a little peek where the shell meets the head to be sure the shrimp are cooked all the way through. While they are still hot, immediately toss the shrimp in a bowl with the cherry tomato halves and the remaining 2 tablespoons of olive oil; mix gently to warm up the tomatoes from the residual heat from the shrimp. This quick step is essential to the dish.

To serve, spoon a mound of the chickpea puree on each of 4 plates, lay 3 shrimp per person on top, spoon some tomatoes around the plate, and let them cascade where they want. Drizzle the shrimp with a bit of the tomato liquid from the mixing bowl and garnish with chives. Serve hot.

chickpea puree

MAKES 2 QUARTS

1/2 pound dried chickpeas/garbanzo beans, picked through and rinsed

2 bay leaves

2 fresh rosemary sprigs plus 1/2 teaspoon chopped fresh rosemary

1 1/2 teaspoons sea salt

1/2 teaspoon freshly ground black pepper, plus additional to taste

1 tablespoon extra-virgin olive oil

Put the dried chickpeas in a large bowl and add cool water to cover by 2 inches. Soak the beans in the refrigerator for at least 18 hours or up to 24; the chickpeas will rehydrate and swell to triple their original size. Drain and rinse thoroughly in a colander.

Transfer the chickpeas to a large pot and cover with fresh water by 2 inches. Toss in the bay leaves and rosemary sprigs; bring gently to a boil over medium heat. Periodically, skim the foam that rises to the top from the chickpeas. Simmer, uncovered, until tender. This can take anywhere from 1 1/2 to 3 hours depending on the age of the bean. When they're done, the chickpeas should be soft and creamy, but not mushy. Season with 1/2 teaspoon of salt only when the beans are cooked through and tender. Remove from the heat and allow the beans to cool in their liquid.

Pull out the bay leaves and rosemary sprigs. Place the pot of beans in a sink full of ice water and stir to cool down or let the beans sit and slowly come to room temperature. Reserve the cooking liquid to use in the puree, which gives great background flavor.

Combine in a pot 1 cup of the softened chickpeas, 1/2 cup of the cooking liquid, the chopped rosemary, 1 teaspoon of the salt, and the pepper; bring to a boil over medium-low heat, skimming if necessary.

Carefully scoop the hot chickpea mixture into a blender; don't fill the blender more than halfway and be sure to hold down the lid with a towel for safety. Puree until smooth and creamy; this should take only a minute since the chickpeas blend so easily when they're hot. Taste, season with salt and pepper, and finish off the puree with the remaining 2 tablespoons of olive oil; blend another few seconds to incorporate. The chickpea puree should be the consistency of a soupy sauce, similar to hummus.

LEFT: GRILLED SHRIMP WITH CHERRY TOMATOES, ROSEMARY, AND CHICKPEA PUREE. ABOVE: LOBSTER TEMPURA WITH TARTAR SAUCE

LOBSTER TEMPURA WITH TARTAR SAUCE SERVES 4

Without a doubt, lobster tempura is our best-selling appetizer. It has appeared on the Lever House menu since the restaurant opened and isn't going anywhere—our guests wouldn't hear of it. This dish is very simple: barely boiled lobster dipped in a light tempura batter, fried, and served with a piquant tartar sauce chock full of shallots, capers, cornichons, and just enough cayenne. . . . What else can be said? I think I'll have one myself!

A few words about cooking lobsters: obviously, at the restaurant, we can use the knuckle and claw meat for other dishes and use the lobster bodies to make stock and sauces . . . we blanch only the tails for this recipe and reserve the other parts for other dishes. When we cook the tails, we separate them from the body and blanch them for two minutes only—you want them set but not totally cooked; they are cooked again when they fry.

4 live lobsters (1½ pounds each)
1 tablespoon sea salt
Ice bath
Canola or other vegetable oil,
    for deep frying
1¾ cups all-purpose flour, plus 1 cup
    for dredging
¾ cup cornstarch
2 tablespoons baking soda
1 tablespoon sugar
1½ teaspoons kosher salt, plus additional
    to taste
2 cups plus 2 tablespoons cold seltzer
Aleppo pepper (see Ingredient Note,
    page 49) or cayenne
2 cups mâche lettuce or baby mixed greens
2 tablespoons Lemon Oil (page 85)
Tartar Sauce (recipe follows)

To cook the lobsters, fill a large stockpot three-quarters of the way with water and add the sea salt; bring to a rapid boil over medium-high heat. Carefully ease 2 of the lobsters into the boiling water, and cook for 2 minutes; they will not be cooked through at this point. Using tongs, carefully remove the lobsters from the pot and plunge them in a large bowl of ice water for at least 5 minutes to ensure they are cool all the way through. Bring the pot of salt water back up to a boil and repeat with the remaining 2 lobsters.

Working with rubber gloves, use a sort of sideways twist to break the legs, claws, and tails off of the bodies; it's best to do this over a sink since it can be messy. (Reserve the bodies for making stock; continue to boil the knuckles, legs, and claws for 5 minutes to cook them fully—serve simply with some squeezed lemon or dip the sweet meat in the tartar sauce.)

Using a big sharp knife, split the tails in half lengthwise. If there are any visible veins or roe along the top of the tail, gently wash them away with cold water. On a work surface, rest the tails on their sides and, using the palm of your hand, press down on them to crack the shells. Break off the outer shells, but keep the actual tails on. Reserve the cleaned tails well wrapped in plastic in the coldest part of the refrigerator until needed. Cleaning and par-boiling the lobsters may be done a day in advance.

In a large heavy pot or deep fryer, heat about 3 inches of vegetable oil to 375°F.

While the oil is heating up, make the tempura batter: In a large bowl, mix 1¾ cups of the flour, the cornstarch, baking soda, sugar, and kosher salt. Whisk in the seltzer until a pancake batter consistency is achieved and there are no lumps. Put the remaining 1 cup of flour on a plate and season well with additional salt and Aleppo pepper.

Before frying the lobster tails, have all of the components of the final dish ready: put a small pile of the mâche lettuce on each of 4 plates, situated at roughly 6 o'clock; drizzle the lettuce with lemon oil. Place a large tablespoon–size dollop of tartar sauce at the top of each plate, at 12 o'clock.

Dust the lobster tails in the seasoned flour to soak up any remaining moisture, shake off the excess. Dip the lobster tails into the batter one by one to lightly coat completely, letting the excess drip back into the bowl.

Holding the lobsters by the tail, gently lower them into the hot oil in batches. Do not over-crowd the pot. The tails should sort of "fizz" when they hit the hot oil and will puff up fairly quickly. Fry the lobster for 2 minutes and then use tongs or chopsticks to turn the pieces over so they cook evenly, about another 2 minutes. When the coating is light golden brown and crisp, carefully remove the tails to a plate lined with paper towels to drain. While the tempura is still hot, lightly season with more salt and Aleppo pepper. Place the lobster tempura on the dressed mâche and serve immediately.

tartar sauce

MAKES ABOUT 1 CUP

1 cup mayonnaise, such as Hellmann's/Best Foods

2 cornichons, drained and finely chopped

2 tablespoons capers, drained, rinsed, and finely chopped

1 shallot, minced

1 tablespoon chopped fresh flat-leaf parsley

1 tablespoon chopped fresh chives

1 tablespoon chopped fresh chervil

Juice of ½ lemon

Pinch of cayenne pepper

3 drops hot sauce, such as Tabasco

Generous pinch of sea salt and freshly ground black pepper

To make the tartar sauce, combine all the ingredients in a mixing bowl and blend well with a wooden spoon. Cover and chill to allow the flavors to marry while preparing the lobster tempura. The tartar sauce tends to lose its punch after a day, so it's best to make it a few hours before you plan to serve it.

Jerusalem artichokes are an underappreciated root vegetable if ever there was one. At Lever House, we include Jerusalem artichokes in our repertoire of vegetables regularly; crispy when raw, nutty when cooked, and a great source of the minerals potassium and phosphorus, Jerusalem artichokes can be cooked in most ways that a potato or artichoke would. Their deep flavor goes perfectly with the sweetness of the scallops and the earthiness of black truffles. Black truffles are a true luxury. If you can find a source for good winter truffles, and can afford the splurge, buy a few ounces and revel in their unique flavor and musky aroma. This soup shows them off in style.

2 tablespoons unsalted butter

1 fennel bulb, sliced

2 celery stalks, sliced

1 large leek, white and pale green parts, washed and sliced (about ½ cup)

Sea salt and freshly ground black pepper

3½ pounds Jerusalem artichokes, unpeeled, well scrubbed, and coarsely chopped (see Ingredient Note)

2 quarts Vegetable Stock (page 228)

½ lime

Scallop Tartare (recipe follows)

Fresh chervil or flat-leaf parsley, for garnish

Shaved black truffles (optional)

Place a soup pot over medium heat and melt the butter. When it begins to foam, add the white mirepoix: the fennel, celery, and leek; season with salt and pepper. Sweat the vegetables in the butter, cook and stir often, until they soften, not brown, about 6 to 7 minutes. Add the chopped Jerusalem artichokes and continue to cook, stirring, for approximately 15 minutes, until the artichokes soften; season with additional salt and pepper to taste.

Pour in the vegetable stock, bring to a boil, reduce to low, and simmer until the Jerusalem artichokes are very tender, about 15 minutes. Skim the soup periodically to remove any impurities that rise to the surface.

Carefully pour the soup into a blender in batches; don't fill the blender more than halfway and be sure to hold down the lid with a towel for safety. Puree until smooth. Taste, season with salt and pepper, and finish off the soup with a little lime juice.

To serve, heat 4 soup bowls. Divide the scallop tartare evenly and place in the center of each bowl, ladle about ¾ cup of the Jerusalem artichoke soup around the scallops, and garnish each serving with a sprig of chervil. If you want to be decadent, shave truffles on top.

INGREDIENT NOTE: JERUSALEM ARTICHOKE
Ironically, the Jerusalem artichoke has no relatives in the actual artichoke family and has nothing whatsoever to do with Jerusalem. The prevalent theory is that Jerusalem derives from *girasole*, the Italian word for sunflower, because this vegetable is, in fact, a member of the sunflower family, which is why you can often find them in the market under the name *sunchokes*. The Jerusalem artichoke is a tuber that grows underground like the potato and looks more like gingerroot than a typical globe artichoke, with the green leaves and prickly heart. Jerusalem artichokes are best in the fall, after the first frost, which for some reason makes them sweeter. When buying the round and knobby root, look for firm, white or brownish, and unblemished tubers. Scrub the tubers well with a vegetable brush. Once cut, they discolor quickly, so put them in water acidulated with lemon juice or vinegar.

scallop tartare

3 large diver scallops (about 6 to 8 ounces), diced

Pinch of fleur de sel

½ tablespoon chopped fresh chives

½ tablespoon black truffle oil

Juice of ¼ lemon

To make the tartare, put the diced scallops in a bowl and add the fleur de sel, chives, truffle oil, and a squeeze of fresh lemon juice; fold the ingredients together gently but thoroughly.

When the chilly days of spring are behind us and before summer really starts, this is a great chilled soup. It starts with a variation on vichyssoise—lots of leeks, potato, and a bit of fennel, all cooked until tender and then pureed with a large handful of sorrel.

The volume measurements for the vegetables and the broth are very important to follow in order to produce the right soup consistency. Sorrel's beguiling citric tang is mellowed and transformed in this soup; its vibrant flavor matches incredibly well with the smoked trout. At the restaurant we garnish the soup with small sourdough croutons and fresh herbs. If you make this soup ahead, give it a big stir before serving because it has a tendency to separate.

6 tablespoons (¾ stick) unsalted butter
1 to 2 large fennel bulbs, sliced (about 2½ cups)
5 leeks, white and pale green parts, washed well and sliced (2 quarts)
Kosher salt and freshly ground black pepper
2 large Idaho potatoes, peeled and sliced thinly (5¼ cups)
10 cups Vegetable Stock (page 228)
Bouquet garni (6 parsley stems, 5 chervil stems, and 2 bay leaves tied together with kitchen string)
½ teaspoon freshly grated nutmeg
7 ounces sorrel, stems removed, washed and dried
1 boneless smoked trout (about 6 to 8 ounces)
Fresh herbs, such as flat-leaf parsley, chervil, tarragon, and dill, for garnish
½ cup small sourdough croutons (optional)

In a large Dutch oven or saucepan over medium heat, melt the butter. When it is foamy, add the fennel and leeks; season lightly with salt and pepper. Sweat the vegetables, stirring occasionally, until they begin to soften, about 15 to 20 minutes.

Fold in the potatoes, season again with salt and pepper, and continue to cook for an additional 10 minutes, until the potatoes begin to soften.

Add the vegetable stock, the bouquet garni, and nutmeg. Bring to a quick boil. Reduce the heat to low and gently simmer for 20 minutes, uncovered, until the vegetables (especially the potatoes) are thoroughly cooked. To test, push a potato against the side of the pot; it should crush very easily.

Add the sorrel, stir well to combine, and remove from the heat immediately. Discard the bouquet garni. Carefully ladle the hot soup into a blender in batches; don't fill the blender more than halfway and be sure to hold down the lid with a towel for safety. Puree until the soup is smooth and a beautiful pastel green.

Pour the soup into another pot. Place the pot in a sink full of ice water and stir to chill the soup quickly. Taste for seasoning when the soup is cold, and adjust as needed. Keep in mind that as the soup chills, the seasoning will become more pronounced.

To serve, break up the pieces of the smoked trout and divide them among chilled soup bowls. Ladle the sorrel soup around the trout, and garnish with fresh-picked herbs. Top the soup with croutons if you wish.

SWEET POTATO AND PEANUT SOUP SERVES 6 TO 8

The combination of sweet, spicy, and nutty—sweet potatoes, chilies, and peanuts—is a bit unusual but very tasty. Feel free to adjust the heat level by altering the amount of jalapeño you add to the soup. To make this rich soup a little more festive, add a spoonful or two of jumbo lump crabmeat seasoned with a squeeze of lime and a bit of salt, just before serving, to provide a heightened new layer of flavor.

1 tablespoon unsalted butter

1 tablespoon canola oil

1 1/2 large Spanish onions, chopped

2 garlic cloves, chopped

1/2 teaspoon Aleppo pepper (see Ingredient Note, page 49) or cayenne

1 tablespoon garam masala or curry powder

1 pound sweet potatoes, peeled and cut into 1/2-inch-thick chunks

5 plum tomatoes, halved and seeded

1 quart Chicken Stock (page 233)

1 1/2 jalapeños, seeded and chopped

1/3 cup smooth peanut butter

Kosher salt and freshly ground black pepper

1/2 lime

2 scallions, green part only, sliced, for garnish

Heat a large Dutch oven or saucepan over medium flame. Add the butter and oil, swirl them around to film the pot. Add the onions, garlic, and Aleppo. Sweat for 10 minutes, stirring occasionally, until the vegetables soften but do not brown. Sprinkle in the garam masala and stir to combine for 1 minute.

Add the sweet potatoes, tomatoes, and stock and simmer gently, uncovered, for 20 minutes, until the sweet potatoes are tender. Add the jalapeños and cook 5 minutes more. Remove from the heat.

Carefully ladle the hot soup into a blender in batches; don't fill the blender more than halfway and be sure to hold down the lid with a towel for safety. Puree until the soup is smooth. Pour the soup into another pot and return to medium heat. Bring the soup to a simmer. Whisk in the peanut butter, until completely incorporated without any clumps. Season lightly with salt and pepper and give a squeeze of lime juice to brighten the finish.

To serve, ladle the soup into warm soup bowls and garnish with scallion.

This hearty soup began its life at Lever House as a request from a local newspaper as an idea for a one-pot meal. After the photo shoot, the staff and I enjoyed digging into big bowls of this boldly flavored soup.

At the restaurant we garnish the white bean soup with a poached egg on top and finish the whole thing off with a drizzle of fruity extra-virgin olive oil and a little sea salt.

When you cut into the egg, the runny yolk oozes into the soup, making it extra luxurious. The addition of the soft poached egg is so delicious that guests have been known to request two eggs on their soup! The dried white beans need to soak in water overnight, so plan accordingly.

1 pound dried cannellini beans, picked through and rinsed

Bouquet garni (1 large leek green, 4 celery leaves, 2 thyme sprigs, and 1 bay leaf tied together with kitchen string)

1½ teaspoons kosher salt, plus additional to taste

2 tablespoons extra-virgin olive oil, plus more for serving

1 pound Palacios chorizo or cured kielbasa, finely diced

2 large Spanish onions, finely diced (about 4 cups)

5 or 6 celery stalks, finely diced (about 2½ cups)

Freshly ground black pepper

1 to 2 bunches green Swiss chard, chiffonade (about 6 cups)

6 to 8 large eggs

1 teaspoon smoked Spanish paprika, for garnish

1 teaspoon fleur de sel, for garnish

Put the beans in a large bowl and add cool water to cover by 2 inches. Soak the beans in the refrigerator for at least 8 hours or overnight. Drain and rinse thoroughly.

Transfer the beans to a medium stockpot. Add the bouquet garni and fresh water to just cover, and bring to a boil. Lower the heat and let simmer until tender, about 1 hour. Periodically, skim the foam that rises to the top.

When done, the beans should be soft and creamy, but not mushy. Season with ½ teaspoon of salt only when they are cooked through and tender. Remove from the heat. Discard the bouquet garni. Strain the beans from their cooking liquid and reserve both. You should have at least 1 quart of cooking liquid.

Film a large Dutch oven or saucepan with 2 tablespoons of oil and place over medium heat. Add the sausage and sauté for 5 minutes, until the oil is a vibrant red color (but don't overbrown the sausage). Add the onion and celery, season with salt and pepper. Sauté until the vegetables are tender, 10 to 12 minutes. Add the reserved beans and stir well to combine, mashing them a bit with the back of a wooden spoon. Pour in 1 quart of the reserved cooking liquid, bring to a boil, and then reduce the heat and gently simmer for about 20 minutes, skimming any froth that rises to the surface.

Stir in the Swiss chard and continue to cook until the chard has wilted into the soup and is tender, about 10 minutes more.

Meanwhile, fill a wide pot with 3 inches of water, add 1 teaspoon of salt, and bring to a gentle simmer over medium-high heat. When the water is just barely bubbling, carefully crack 2 or 3 eggs into it, spacing them apart. Poach for 3 minutes, until just cooked but the yolks are still soft. Remove the eggs with a slotted spoon to a plate and dab the bottom of the eggs with paper towels to blot dry. Repeat with the remaining eggs.

Ladle the hot soup into warm bowls, place a poached egg on top, and sprinkle the egg with a little paprika and fleur de sel. Drizzle the soup with a few drops of olive oil.

Although we favor large or jumbo asparagus for this salad, if you prefer the pencil-thin ones, then by all means use them, just don't peel them. What's great about this peasant-style salad is the textural contrast between the cooked asparagus and the finely shaved raw ones. Marcona almonds and Manchego cheese give this satisfying salad a slightly Spanish slant, and the sharpness of the cheese and the crunch of the nuts accent the roasted asparagus perfectly. Marcona almonds are large, flat nuts that are more buttery and rich than the normal American variety. Addictive, to be sure!

20 large asparagus spears (about
1½ bunches)
2 tablespoons extra-virgin olive oil
Kosher salt and freshly ground black pepper
¼ pound baby arugula, rinsed and dried
½ cup marcona almonds, lightly toasted
¼ cup Sherry-Dijon Vinaigrette
(recipe follows)
4 ounces Manchego cheese, shaved

Preheat the oven to 400°F.

Cut or snap off about 1 inch of the tough bottom stem of the asparagus and discard. Set aside 4 of the asparagus spears. With the remaining 16 spears, use a vegetable peeler and shave off the outer skin of the lower half of the remaining stalk, keeping the tops intact. Put these spears in a mixing bowl and coat with the oil; season with salt and pepper. Spread out the asparagus in a single layer on a sheet pan. Roast the asparagus for 10 minutes, until tender but not brown. Reserve the roasted asparagus at room temperature.

Shave the remaining raw asparagus spears into long ribbons using a vegetable peeler or mandolin. Fill a mixing bowl with ice water and soak the asparagus ribbons in it for about 5 minutes to crisp them up. Put the shaved asparagus in a salad spinner or pat with paper towels to dry well.

In a large bowl, combine the arugula, shaved asparagus ribbons, and almonds; season with salt and pepper. Dress the salad with about ¼ cup of the sherry-Dijon vinaigrette (salads are best well dressed, where each leaf is filmed with vinaigrette, *not drenched*). Toss the ingredients gently using your hands to combine.

To serve, arrange 4 spears of the roasted asparagus on each of 4 plates. Put a large handful of the salad on top, trying to equally distribute the arugula and the goodies for each portion.

Sprinkle the shaved Manchego on top of the salads and finish off with a final grind of black pepper.

sherry-dijon vinaigrette

MAKES ¾ CUP

2 large shallots, finely diced
Generous pinch of kosher salt
1 tablespoon Dijon mustard
2 tablespoons sherry vinegar
½ cup extra-virgin olive oil
Generous pinch of freshly ground black pepper

To prepare a quick vinaigrette for the asparagus, put the diced shallots in a medium mixing bowl and sprinkle with a healthy pinch of salt. Let them sit for 5 minutes to allow the salt to draw out the water from the shallots; this will ultimately help hold together the vinaigrette. Add the mustard and vinegar and whisk with the shallots to combine. Slowly add the oil in a stream while whisking to emulsify the vinaigrette. Add a pinch of ground black pepper to balance it out. Keep any leftover vinaigrette covered in the refrigerator for up to 3 days.

MARINATED PORTUGUESE SARDINES WITH TOMATO-FENNEL COMPOTE SERVES 4

These cured sardines are a big hit at Lever House as an appetizer. If you can get your hands on fresh sardines, this is a marvelous way to highlight them. You can vary the aromatics in the cure to suit your personal taste. If you don't like the licorice flavor of fennel seeds and star anise, go ahead and substitute coriander seeds or fresh thyme. You could even omit the aromatics altogether, cure the sardines with salt alone, marinate them in good extra-virgin olive oil, and savor the unadulterated oceany goodness of the sardines. They can also be served on bread toasts as crostini for a party; simply slather the bread with some tomato-fennel compote, lay the marinated sardines on top, and garnish with fennel fronds. It takes time for the cure to penetrate the sardines, so think ahead. The tomato-fennel compote is also ideal to toss with hot pasta, topped with grated Parmesan, for a quick dinner. And you can mix the compote with Chickpea Puree (page 69) for an interesting vegetarian dip.

1 cup kosher salt

1 tablespoon fennel seed, coarsely ground

1 whole star anise, finely ground

1½ pounds small whole sardines (about 8),
   filleted

1 lemon, thinly sliced

2 bay leaves, halved

2 fresh thyme sprigs

⅛ teaspoon red pepper flakes

About ½ cup extra-virgin olive oil or more
   to cover

½ to ¾ cup Tomato-Fennel Compote (recipe
   follows)

Freshly ground black pepper

Mix the salt, ground fennel seed, and star anise in a small bowl to distribute evenly. Sprinkle a glass baking dish with half of the salt mixture and arrange the sardines on top in a single layer, flesh side down. Sprinkle the remaining salt cure over the sardines, cover with plastic wrap, and refrigerate for 2 hours, until the fillets firm up a bit.

Rinse the sardine fillets with cool running water and pat dry with paper towels. Put the sardines in a 13 × 9-inch glass or plastic container in a single layer, lay the lemon slices on top, then the bay leaves, thyme, and a light sprinkle of red pepper flakes. Pour the olive oil over the sardines to submerge completely. Cover with plastic wrap and allow to marinate in the refrigerator for 8 hours or up to overnight before serving. As long as the sardines are completely covered with oil, they will keep for 3 or 4 days in the fridge.

To serve, lay 2 sardine fillets next to each other on a plate, crisscross 2 more fillets across them so you have an X. Put a spoonful of the tomato-fennel compote in the empty space at the top of the X. Drizzle the plates with some of the olive oil from the sardines and garnish with the fennel fronds reserved when making the compote. Finish off the dish with a grind of fresh black pepper.

tomato-fennel compote

MAKES 2 CUPS

3 tablespoons extra-virgin olive oil

1 fennel bulb, finely diced, fennel fronds
   reserved for garnish

Kosher salt and freshly ground black pepper

2 bunches scallions, green parts only, finely
   chopped

1 (8.5-ounce) jar sun-dried tomatoes packed
   in oil

1 tablespoon good-quality balsamic vinegar

Place a small sauté pan over medium heat and coat with the oil. When the oil gets hazy, add the diced fennel and sauté for 5 to 8 minutes, until the fennel is tender but not browned; season with salt and pepper. Add the scallions, stirring to mix well, and cook until the scallions wilt and just become soft, only about 1 minute. Refrigerate the mixture until chilled.

Meanwhile, blend the sun-dried tomatoes and their oil in a food processor and pulse until the tomatoes are finely ground. Scrape the ground tomatoes into a medium mixing bowl; add the chilled fennel/scallion mixture and the balsamic vinegar. Mix well and season with salt and pepper.

HEIRLOOM TOMATO SALAD WITH LEMON OIL SERVES 4

The main attraction in this salad is featuring local heirloom tomatoes in peak season, which is summer to early fall. The sweetness of the ripened tomatoes defines the integrity of the salad.

It honestly doesn't matter how many varieties of tomatoes you use; the most important thing is that the tomatoes are juicy and sweet, otherwise don't waste your time making this recipe. Buy more than you need. Make BLTs. Make tomato sauce. Enjoy tomatoes while they are at their best and then don't make this salad again until next summer.

Lemon oil is also great to have around to use at will, drizzle on a piece of grilled fish, or use instead of regular olive oil in vinaigrettes. The lemon essence takes a little time to steep into the oil, so think about knocking it out the night before you want to use it.

1 small red onion, thinly sliced

2 slices sourdough bread, crust removed, cut into small cubes, about ⅛-inch pieces

Kosher salt and freshly ground black pepper

2 tablespoons extra-virgin olive oil

4 to 8 assorted ripe heirloom tomatoes, such as brandywine, green zebra, sungold, and red beefsteak

¼ cup Lemon Oil (recipe follows)

12 small Italian basil leaves

Maldon sea salt (see Ingredient Note) or fleur de sel and freshly ground black pepper

2 teaspoons balsamic or sherry vinegar (optional)

Fill a medium mixing bowl with ice water and soak the onion slices for about 15 minutes to crisp them up and mellow some of their potent flavor. Put the onions in a salad spinner or pat with paper towels to dry well.

To make the croutons, preheat the oven to 350°F. Put the bread cubes in a bowl, season with salt and pepper, and toss with the olive oil to coat. Spread the bread cubes on a sheet pan and bake for 5 minutes, until light golden brown. Set aside to cool to room temperature.

Cut the bigger tomatoes in ¼-inch-thick slices and quarter or halve the smaller ones; this salad looks great with different colored tomatoes of varying sizes and shapes. We cannot stress enough the importance of using ripe tomatoes!

To serve, arrange the tomato slices among 4 chilled plates, lay a few pieces of onion on top of the tomatoes, and drizzle about 1 tablespoon of lemon oil over each serving of tomatoes. Scatter a few basil leaves and croutons on the salads. Season with sea salt and pepper; add a couple drops of good balsamic or sherry vinegar if you like.

lemon oil

MAKES 2 CUPS

2 cups extra-virgin olive oil

2 lemons, rinsed and halved

1 bay leaf

¼ teaspoon whole black peppercorns

1 small dried red chili

In a medium saucepan over low heat, combine the oil, lemon halves, bay leaf, peppercorns, and red chili; the lemon tends to take on a bitterness if it gets too hot. Bring to a slow simmer, just until the lemons begin to produce small bubbles in the oil, about 20 to 30 minutes. "Low and slow" is the key method here. Do not allow the oil to boil or become too hot; you don't want to fry the ingredients, just infuse the oil with the aromatics.

Remove the pot from the heat and allow the oil to cool at room temperature for about 1 hour. Pour the oil, along with all the aromatics, into a container, cover, and refrigerate for 8 hours or up to overnight; the flavors of the lemon and pepper will steep into the oil as it sits.

The next day, strain the lemon oil through a fine sieve to remove the solid pieces. Reserve the lemon oil, covered and refrigerated, for up to 1 week.

INGREDIENT NOTE: MALDON SEA SALT

At the restaurant, we use Maldon sea salt on this fresh tomato salad for its superior texture and clean flavor. The soft flaky crystals are delicate enough to crumble easily between the fingers and have a totally different taste from regular grains of table salt. This English sea salt is completely natural and without artificial additives; it's sold at specialty markets and some grocery stores. Good salt can make all the difference when cooking. Salt can bring out the natural flavors of food, rather than just making it taste salty. Most people don't season enough.

The slow-roasted tomatoes take a little time in the oven, but it's basically unattended labor. To get them out of the way, so you don't have to rush the slow-roasting process, it is convenient to make them the day before you plan to serve the salad. The recipe can easily be doubled or tripled, and the dried tomatoes keep in the refrigerator for at least a week. Have the slow-roasted tomatoes on hand to use at will; they are great to put on sandwiches or toss with pasta. Make a batch at the end of summer when there are lots of ripe tomatoes around. It is also ideal to make in the middle of winter, when the tomatoes won't be good to eat raw.

Roasting the tomatoes draws out water and concentrates the tomato's sunny flavor.

10 plum tomatoes, halved lengthwise, seeds removed
1 teaspoon sea salt
1 teaspoon fresh thyme leaves
1/2 teaspoon ground anise seed
2 garlic cloves, thickly sliced (about 10 slices total)
6 tablespoons extra-virgin olive oil, plus more to cover
60 fennel seeds
40 salt-packed capers, rinsed and drained

1 fennel bulb, trimmed, halved, and very thinly sliced, fennel fronds reserved for garnish
2 tablespoons good-quality balsamic vinegar
2 cups baby spinach, rinsed and dried
Kosher salt and freshly ground black pepper

To make the slow-roasted tomatoes, preheat the oven to 275°F. For ease, line a baking sheet with parchment paper or foil, so the tomatoes won't stick to the pan.

Put the tomatoes in a large bowl, add the sea salt, thyme, anise, garlic, and 2 tablespoons of oil; toss with your hands to combine. Arrange the tomatoes on the prepared pan, in a single layer, cut side up. Bake for 3 hours to dehydrate them, until they have shrunken and are dry to the touch; rotate the pan halfway through cooking. Cool the oven-dried tomatoes, remove any pieces of garlic, and then peel off the skin.

Put the tomatoes in a nonreactive container and top each one with 3 fennel seeds and 2 capers. Pour olive oil over the tomatoes to cover them completely and top with a lid. The tomatoes may be stored in the refrigerator a few days before serving. The tomato oil is great for dipping bread or for using in the salad.

To prepare the salad, fill a mixing bowl with ice water and soak the fennel slices for about 15 minutes to crisp them up. Put the fennel in a salad spinner or pat with paper towels to dry well.

In a small bowl, whisk together the balsamic vinegar and remaining 4 tablespoons of oil to make a vinaigrette, or use the tomato oil for added flavor. Combine the fennel slices and spinach in a mixing bowl and toss with the vinaigrette; season with a generous amount of salt and pepper.

To serve, arrange 5 tomato "petals" on each of 4 plates in a star shape, leaving a space in the middle to put the salad. Pile a handful of the spinach-fennel salad in the center of the tomatoes and garnish with fennel fronds. Season with additional salt and pepper.

WILD MUSHROOM AND LEEK FLAN WITH SHAVED WHITE TRUFFLES SERVES 4

This savory custard is a take on the classic dish from the Piedmont region of northern Italy, where one of Italy's great wines, Barolo, is also produced. The cuisine of this area is a dynamic blend of Italian mountain specialties and strong Gallic flavors influenced by its proximity to France and Switzerland.

It is common to see indigenous ingredients like white truffles and porcini mushrooms in Piedmontese recipes. Fresh white truffles are always expensive. In some years their prices defy rational explanation. The truffle hunter's rule of thumb is that a good truffle year is a bad year for wine—wet summers are good for truffles, but bad for wine grapes. People who appreciate white truffles (and can afford them) will pay just about anything to enjoy their intoxicating and sensual fragrance.

This recipe celebrates the marriage of white truffles, leeks, wild mushrooms, and cream—ingredients that partner well with both white and black truffles. Please don't be put off if you can't find or afford truffles. Make the flan anyway and it's still an attention-getter (a drizzle of a little white truffle oil will do the trick!).

4 tablespoons unsalted butter

1 large leek, white and pale green parts, washed and finely chopped

1/2 pound assorted mushrooms, such as porcini, chanterelle, cremini, and shiitake, finely chopped

1 3/4 cups heavy cream

1/2 cup milk

Bouquet garni (2 rosemary sprigs, 2 sage leaves, and 2 bay leaves tied with kitchen string)

3 large eggs, beaten

1/2 cup coarsely grated Parmigiano-Reggiano

1/8 teaspoon freshly grated nutmeg

Pinch of cayenne

Kosher salt and freshly ground black pepper

1 cup micro greens or baby mixed greens

Shaved white truffles or white truffle oil (optional)

Heat a large sauté pan over medium flame and add 2 tablespoons of the butter. When the butter begins to foam, add the leeks and mushrooms and sauté until the vegetables are tender and their moisture has evaporated, about 10 minutes. Set aside to cool to room temperature.

In a small saucepan over medium-low flame, combine the cream, milk, and bouquet garni. Bring the cream to a brief simmer, stirring occasionally; take care not to let the cream come to a full boil in order to prevent it from spilling over. Turn off the heat and allow the herbs to steep in the dairy for 1 hour to infuse the flavor. Strain the cream mixture and reserve at room temperature.

Preheat the oven to 350°F. Bring a kettle of water to a boil for the water bath and keep it hot.

Melt the remaining 2 tablespoons of butter and lightly brush it on the bottom and sides of four 4-ounce ramekins; put them in the refrigerator to set for 5 minutes.

In a large bowl, whisk together the cream mixture, mushrooms and leeks, eggs, cheese, nutmeg, cayenne, salt, and pepper until well combined. Place the buttered ramekins in a small baking pan and ladle the mixture into the molds. Add enough hot water to the pan to come halfway up the sides of the ramekins; be careful not to get water into the custard. Carefully transfer the pan to the middle oven rack, and bake for 20 to 30 minutes, until the custard is barely set and just jiggles slightly. Allow the flans to cool in the water bath.

To serve, run a thin knife around the inside of each ramekin to loosen the flans, place a plate on top of each, and invert to pop them out. Mound a small amount of the greens in the center of each flan and shave lots and lots of fresh white truffles over the top . . . enjoy the experience. (Alternatively, drizzle with white truffle oil.) The mushroom and leek flans may be served hot or at room temperature if you prefer. For ease, they can also be made a few hours in advance and then simply warmed in the oven before serving.

BRAISED PORK BELLY WITH SOUBISE SERVES 4

Pork belly is basically uncured fresh bacon; it is God's gift to all who partake. Pork in general responds well to brining, as it promotes juicier and more flavorful meat. Like a marinade, brining keeps food succulent and increases the ability of the meat to hold moisture. This is a versatile all-purpose brine that works well on poultry, such as turkey and chicken. There is not a great deal of salt in the brine recipe, since salt tends to break down the fibers of the meat, making it a tad mushy and overly salty if left too long. It's ideal to brine the pork the night before you plan on serving, although the amount of time is not set in stone; even a little brining is better than none.

Soubise is a rich, velvety white sauce that is a savory accompaniment to roasted meats, especially good with pork. It always contains lots of soft, slow-cooked onions. It is of key importance that the onions do not brown or caramelize for this sauce; they should be moist and soft, not charred in the slightest. This process takes love and time, so, to give the onions the proper attention, make the soubise the night before. This dish is not as challenging as it looks.

BRINE

1 quart water

¼ cup sugar

2½ tablespoons sea salt

2 bay leaves

5 juniper berries, smashed

3 garlic cloves, smashed

1 teaspoon red pepper flakes

1 pound pork belly, without rind

Generous pinch of kosher salt and
   freshly ground black pepper

BRAISE

2 tablespoons canola oil

1 onion, coarsely chopped

1 celery stalk, coarsely chopped

1 carrot, coarsely chopped

½ fennel bulb, coarsely chopped

3 garlic cloves, coarsely chopped

2 fresh thyme sprigs

2 bay leaves

1 teaspoon whole black peppercorns

1 cup dry white wine, such as Sauvignon
   Blanc

1 quart Brown Veal Stock (page 230)

Kosher salt and freshly ground black pepper

1 cup Soubise (recipe follows), warmed

2 tablespoons chopped fresh chives,
   for garnish

To prepare the brine, in a large container, combine the water, sugar, sea salt, bay leaves, juniper, garlic, and red pepper flakes. Give it a stir to dissolve the sugar and salt. Submerge the pork belly in the brine, cover, and put it in the refrigerator for 8 hours or up to overnight to tenderize the meat.

Remove the pork belly from the brine and pat dry with paper towels. Sprinkle both sides of the meat with a fair amount of salt and pepper. Preheat the oven to 325°F.

To braise the pork, place a cast-iron or deep ovenproof skillet over medium-high heat and coat with the oil. When the oil gets hazy, add the pork belly and sear for 3 minutes on each side, until the meat is brown and the fat begins to render. Remove the seared pork belly to a side plate and tip out all but 2 tablespoons of the rendered fat. Reduce the heat to medium and add the mirepoix to the pan: the onion, celery, carrot, fennel, and garlic; toss in the thyme, bay leaves, and peppercorns. Sweat the vegetables in the pork fat, cook and stir often, until they soften, not brown, about 15 minutes.

Add the wine and continue to cook for 5 minutes, until the liquid is reduced to ¼ cup and looks syrupy. Turn the heat up to high, add the veal stock, and bring to a boil, skimming any impurities that may rise to the surface.

Return the pork belly to the pan; the liquid should just barely cover the meat. Cover the pan tightly with foil and transfer to the hot oven to braise for 2 to 2½ hours, or until the pork is very tender and a fork slides into the meat without any resistance. Allow the pork belly to cool in the braising liquid, preferably overnight, covered in the refrigerator.

The next day, remove the pork belly from the braising liquid, scraping away all solids that stick to the meat.

Preheat the oven to 425°F and put a dry cast-iron or ovenproof skillet in the oven to preheat at the same time.

Using a sharp knife, divide the pork into 4 equal portions (it is easier to cut when it's cool). Season the pieces of pork belly lightly with salt and pepper, and put them in a single layer in the preheated pan. Roast for 10 minutes, until the meat is tender, but not falling apart and the fat is crispy.

To serve, ladle ¼ cup of the soubise sauce on each of 4 plates, put a piece of the pork belly in the center, and shower with chopped chives.

soubise

MAKES ABOUT 2 CUPS

2 tablespoons vegetable oil

1½ pounds white onions, finely diced

1 lemon thyme sprig

1 bay leaf

Kosher salt and freshly ground black pepper

¾ cup dry white wine, such as Sauvignon Blanc

½ cup white wine vinegar

1 cup Vegetable or Chicken Stock (page 228 and 233), as needed

¼ cup (½ stick) unsalted butter, cold and cut in chunks

Place a saucepan over medium heat and film with the oil. When the oil is hazy, add the onions, thyme, and bay leaf; season with salt and pepper. Cook and stir for 5 minutes, until fragrant, but do not let them brown.

Add the wine and vinegar, bring to a simmer, then cover and reduce the heat to low. Simmer gently for 3 hours, checking periodically to make sure the liquid has not completely evaporated and that the onions are soupy; add stock a little at a time to keep the onions moist if needed.

Remove the thyme sprig and bay leaf, and while the onions are still hot, transfer to a blender. Pulse the soft onions until slightly chunky. Add the butter in increments and continue to pulse until the butter melts into the hot onions and the sauce reduces to a puree. Adjust seasoning with salt and pepper. The sauce may be made a day in advance and gently reheated on the stovetop before serving.

ENTRÉES

I think the entrées on the menu at Lever House offer a wide array of choices for guests. The recipes we've chosen for the book offer a similarly wide variety, from simple meat and fish dishes to more demanding recipes that require additional time and effort. All are packed with flavor. Although some of the recipes may seem complex, once you have prepared the mise en place for a dish—assembled the dish's building blocks—the actual assembly/preparation times tend to be relatively short.

Use the best-quality meats and the freshest fish you can find. Also, if you do not like (or cannot locate ingredients for) the vegetable accompaniments that a certain dish calls for, check the "Sides" section of the book and substitute another vegetable that is more to your taste or is readily available.

Chatham or Atlantic cod is an often over-looked fish. When it is pristinely fresh, it can be a revelation. Beautifully firm, white, flaky cod with meltingly sweet onion confit and a tangy black olive sauce is a fulfilling combination. At the restaurant we favor distinctive and delicious alfonso olives for this sauce, which hail from Chile. The large purple salty gems of fruit have a soft bite that bursts of briny red wine. This savory dish is fast and flavorful. Make the onion confit a day in advance to save time while also allowing the flavors to mellow out; gently reheat before serving. Please allow yourself enough time to cook down the onions slowly. If they cook too quickly, they will stick and burn, marring the golden color created when you cook them gently. We often serve this dish with crispy polenta to add a bit of crunch to the plate.

4 Chatham or Atlantic cod fillets (6 ounces each), skin on
Kosher salt and freshly ground black pepper
2 tablespoons canola oil
1 cup Onion Confit (recipe follows)
1 cup Black Olive Sauce (recipe follows)
Fresh basil, for garnish

Season the cod lightly on both sides with salt and pepper. Place a large sauté pan over high flame, and coat with the oil. When the oil gets hazy, carefully lay the cod fillets in the pan, skin side down, and sear for 4 minutes without moving them around to help form a crisp crust. Carefully flip over the fish and cook the other side for another 3 minutes.

To serve, place about ¼ cup of the onion confit in the center of 4 large plates, using a slotted spoon. Ladle the black olive sauce around the onions, and lay a piece of cod, skin side up, on the onion confit; garnish each portion with a basil leaf.

onion confit

MAKES ABOUT 2 CUPS

3 large Spanish onions (about 3 pounds),
   thinly sliced

1 teaspoon sea salt

2 tablespoons water

In a saucepan over low heat, combine the onions, salt, and water. Stir well and slowly heat, covered, until the onions are very tender, about 2 hours; stirring occasionally as not to burn the bottom. The longer and slower you stew the onions, the sweeter and softer they become. Uncover and continue to cook and stir for about 20 minutes, or until the liquid in the pan has evaporated and reduced to a syrup. The onions will take on a lovely golden hue. Onion confit may be made a day in advance and gently reheated before serving.

black olive sauce

MAKES ABOUT 1¼ CUPS

½ cup pitted alfonso olives

1 tablespoon chopped fresh rosemary needles

1 tablespoon chopped fresh marjoram leaves

¾ cup Vegetable Stock (page 228)

2 tablespoons unsalted butter

½ tablespoon store-bought red wine mustard
   or ¾ teaspoon each Dijon and balsamic
   vinegar mixed together

Combine the olives, rosemary, marjoram, and stock in a small stainless-steel pot and bring to a boil over medium heat. Once the olive mixture starts to bubble, add the butter and turn off the heat. Carefully ladle the hot mixture into a blender in batches; don't fill the blender more than halfway and be sure to hold down the lid with a towel for safety. Puree until smooth. Add the mustard and blend for 5 seconds to incorporate. Strain the sauce and reserve warm.

Provençal cuisine is almost always prepared with olive oil and garlic. Tomatoes are another common ingredient; in fact, you can safely assume that any dish described as *"à la provençale"* will be a medley of tomatoes, squash, and peppers, just as it is here. The Provençal vegetables take a little while to marinate, so get the recipe going in the morning or the night before. Although it takes a little extra time, once you have the vegetables set, putting together the rest of this dish is a snap.

Marinated Provençal Vegetables (recipe follows)

1 cup liquid reserved from marinated vegetables (recipe follows) or Nage (page 57)

Pinch of saffron threads

2 tablespoons sherry vinegar

¼ cup plus 2 tablespoons extra-virgin olive oil

Kosher salt and freshly ground black pepper

1½ pounds sushi-quality tuna loin, cut into 4 pieces

Chopped fresh chives and basil, for garnish

Prepare the marinated Provençal vegetables.

In a blender, combine the 1 cup vegetable liquid, ¾ cup of the marinated Provençal vegetables, and the saffron; puree at high speed until completely smooth. Add the vinegar and then with the motor running, slowly pour in ¼ cup of the olive oil. The vinaigrette should have nice acidity. Adjust with salt and pepper. Reserve cold.

Pat the tuna dry with paper towels and sprinkle all sides with a fair amount of salt and pepper—you should see the seasoning on the meat. Heat a grill pan or cast-iron skillet over medium flame. Rub the fish with the remaining 2 tablespoons of oil. Lay the tuna in the hot pan and sear for about 1½ minutes on each side to form a crust; as the tuna cooks, the red meat will become whiter; grill for a total of 5 to 6 minutes for rare. Transfer the tuna to a cutting board and cut on a slight angle into 1-inch slices.

To serve, for a supreme presentation, set a 3-inch ring mold in the center of a small plate and spoon a quarter of the marinated Provençal vegetables into it to fill; press down gently with the back of a spoon to hold the vegetables together. Carefully remove the ring, so the vegetables keep their round shape; repeat with the remaining servings. Alternatively, simply spoon a pile of the vegetables on each of 4 plates. Fan the tuna slices around the vegetables, drizzle the tuna with the vinaigrette, and garnish with a shower of chives and basil.

marinated provençal vegetables

MAKES ABOUT 6 CUPS

2 tomatoes
½ fennel bulb, diced
1 small zucchini, diced
1 yellow squash, such as goldbar, diced
1 red bell pepper, seeded and diced
1 green bell pepper, seeded and diced
1 yellow bell pepper, seeded and diced
6 tablespoons extra-virgin olive oil
1 large Spanish onion, diced
3 fresh thyme sprigs
3 fresh basil leaves
3 bay leaves
2 garlic cloves, smashed
¼ cup black olives, such as niçoise,
    pitted and chopped
¼ cup green olives, such as Sicilian,
    pitted and chopped
2 tablespoons capers, drained, rinsed,
    and chopped
Pinch of saffron threads
½ teaspoon red pepper flakes
Kosher salt and freshly ground black pepper

Bring a large pot of water to a boil.

Prepare the tomatoes by making a small X in the bottoms with a paring knife, scoring the skin but not cutting through too deep. Place the tomatoes in boiling water and cook for 10 to 15 seconds depending on ripeness. When the skin starts to peel away from the flesh of the tomato, remove from the boiling water with a slotted spoon and plunge in an ice bath to "shock" them, or cool them down right away. Drain and peel off the skins with your fingers. Cut the tomatoes in half, squeeze out the seeds, and dice the flesh.

Bring the water back up to a boil. Blanch and shock the rest of the vegetables in order (the fennel, zucchini and yellow squash, and bell peppers) in 3 separate batches, so the colors and flavors stay true and individual. Use a slotted spoon to remove the vegetables from the water. Put all the blanched Provençal vegetables in a large bowl.

Heat a sauté pan over medium flame and coat with 2 tablespoons of oil. When the oil is hot, add the onion, and sweat for 5 minutes, just until soft but without color. Cool for a few minutes, then scrape the sautéed onion into the bowl of blanched vegetables.

Toss the thyme, basil, bay leaves, and garlic into the vegetable mixture. Mix in the black and green olives, capers, saffron, red pepper flakes, and remaining 4 tablespoons of oil; season lightly with salt and pepper. Cover and marinate 4 hours or up to overnight, tossing occasionally.

Pick out the herbs and garlic pieces before using the vegetable mixture. The marinated Provençal vegetables may be served cold or at room temperature.

To make the vinaigrette for the tuna, drain and reserve the liquid from the vegetable mixture and reserve ¾ cup of the mixture itself to puree in the recipe.

Hake is without a doubt one of my favorite fish. A cousin of cod, but with a meatier texture and firmer flake, hake is a slender, somewhat scaly fish. It stands up well to the herbaceous salsa verde, which helps bring into sharp focus the flavors of the fish and mild vegetables. The salsa verde can be made ahead of time but is best when assembled at the last minute.

½ pound salsify (see Ingredient Note)

1 lemon, halved

1½ tablespoons extra-virgin olive oil

1½ tablespoons unsalted butter

1 pound oyster mushrooms

1 tablespoon chopped fresh flat-leaf parsley

Kosher salt and freshly ground black pepper

4 hake fillets (6 ounces each)

Pinch of cayenne

½ cup Salsa Verde (recipe follows)

Peel the salsify (you may want to wear gloves) and put them in a bowl of water acidulated with the juice of ½ lemon to prevent discoloration. Bring a large pot of lightly salted water to a boil and add the juice of the remaining ½ lemon. Simmer the salsify, uncovered, for 15 minutes, until al dente. Remove the salsify from the pot with tongs and put on a cutting board to cool. Slice the salsify on the bias into ¼-inch pieces.

Place a large sauté pan over medium heat and add the oil and butter. When the butter has melted, add the oyster mushrooms all at once; raise the heat to medium-high and cook, stirring occasionally, until the mushroom liquid evaporates and the mushrooms begin to brown, about 6 minutes. When they are caramelized, add the parsley and season well with

salt and pepper. Fold in the salsify and toss to incorporate and heat through. Remove the pan from the heat and cover it to keep warm while preparing the fish.

Place a large nonstick pan over medium heat. Season the hake on both sides with a pinch of salt, pepper to taste, and the cayenne. Lay the fish fillets in the pan and sear for 3 minutes on each side, until golden brown.

To serve, divide the mushroom-salsify mixture among 4 plates, lay a hake fillet on top of the vegetables, and drizzle some salsa verde over the fish.

INGREDIENT NOTE: SALSIFY

A member of the sunflower family, salsify is also known as oyster plant because its taste is reminiscent of a delicately flavored oyster. This long root vegetable resembles a thin parsnip with creamy white skin covered with grasslike sprouts. A native of Central and Southern Europe, salsify is harvested in the fall to be enjoyed through the winter as a cooked vegetable. Look for firm, plump unblemished roots and store them in the refrigerator for up to a week. Cook and serve salsify as you would parsnips. Gloves may be in order when you work with the salsify, to avoid discoloration of your hands.

salsa verde

MAKES ABOUT 1 CUP

1 cup fresh flat-leaf parsley leaves, firmly packed, washed and dried

3 tablespoons salt-packed capers, soaked in water for 10 minutes, drained, and dried

3 garlic cloves, coarsely chopped

½ teaspoon red pepper flakes

½ cup extra-virgin olive oil

1 tablespoon sherry wine vinegar

6 tablespoons sourdough bread crumbs

1 teaspoon fleur de sel

Put the parsley, capers, garlic, and pepper flakes in a food processor. Pulse until the mixture is coarsely combined. Pour in the oil and pulse a few more times to incorporate. The salsa verde should be wet and slightly soupy in consistency. Stir in the sherry vinegar and scrape the salsa verde into a bowl. Fold in the bread crumbs and fleur de sel just before serving.

HALIBUT WITH ROASTED BABY BEETS, CIPOLLINI ONIONS, AND FINES HERBES   SERVES 4

I'll never understand why people don't like beets . . . roasted beets are wonderfully sweet

and have a great texture. Golden and candy-striped (chioggia) beets are visually striking, and

they are devoid of the bitterness generally associated with red beets. Fines herbes is a mix-

ture of finely chopped fresh herbs that are usually added to a dish right before serving. The

consistency and color is similar to an Italian pesto or French pistou. In this dish, the pounded

herb mixture releases the most wonderful fragrance when stirred into the

beet-and-cipollini-onion mixture. It's ideal to make the

pounded herbs in a mortar and pestle, adding

the herbs a bit at a time, although

alternatively, you can make them

in a food processor. Pounded fines

herbes are also excellent spread on

slices of grilled sourdough bread with a

glass of crisp white wine.

1 bunch baby candy-striped beets (chioggia), about ½ pound, unpeeled, all but 1 inch of tops trimmed, rinsed (see Ingredient Note)

1 bunch baby golden beets, about ½ pound, unpeeled, all but 1 inch of tops trimmed, rinsed

¼ cup extra-virgin olive oil

Kosher salt and freshly ground black pepper

4 whole star anise

½ pound cipollini onions, peeled

1 cup Nage (page 57)

3 tablespoons unsalted butter

4 halibut fillets (6 ounces each)

Pinch of cayenne

2 tablespoons canola oil

2 tablespoons Pounded Fines Herbes (recipe follows)

Fresh chervil or flat-leaf parsley, for garnish

Preheat the oven to 375°F.

Place the beets in a small roasting pan or glass baking dish and toss with 2 tablespoons of olive oil to coat; season well with salt and pepper. Arrange the beets in a single layer and pour in enough water, about ½ cup, to reach about a quarter of the way up the sides of the beets. Scatter the star anise on top and cover the pan tightly with foil. Roast the beets until they are tender, about 30 to 40 minutes, depending on the size and freshness of the beets.

Once the beets get a head start in the oven, put the onions in a mixing bowl and toss with the remaining 2 tablespoons of olive oil to coat; season well with salt and pepper. Put the onions on a small sheet pan on the other rack of the oven, and roast for 15 to 25 minutes, just until tender and beginning to color. Cool to room temperature and reserve.

To check for doneness of the beets, insert a paring knife into the centers; it should slide in without any resistance. Allow the beets to cool, and then slip off the skins using your hands. Cut the beets in half or in quarters, depending on their size.

Warm the nage in a saucepan over medium heat; add the beets, onions, and butter. Let it slowly come to a simmer; season lightly with salt and pepper.

While the beets and onions are heating up in the liquid, season the halibut with salt, pepper, and cayenne. Place a large sauté pan over medium-high heat and coat with the canola oil. Add the halibut fillets and cook until the bottom side is golden, about 2 to 3 minutes. Flip over the fish and cook the other side for another 2 to 3 minutes; the fish should be just cooked through and buttery, not dry in the slightest.

When the vegetables are heated through, stir in 2 tablespoons of the pounded fines herbes. Ladle a scoop of the vegetables and herb-infused nage into each of 4 bowls (you can preheat them if you'd like). Lay the seared halibut fillet on top of the beet-onion mixture; it should be resting in the broth, not submerged. Garnish with sprigs of chervil.

pounded fines herbes

MAKES ABOUT 1 CUP

½ cup fresh chervil leaves and very fine stems only

2 tablespoons fresh tarragon leaves

½ cup fresh flat-leaf parsley leaves

Kosher salt

½ to ¾ cup extra-virgin olive oil

Toss together the chervil, tarragon, and parsley. In a mortar and pestle, begin pounding a quarter of the herbs with 1 tablespoon of kosher salt, add a little of the olive oil, and continue to pound the herbs to a green paste. Add a little sprinkle of salt and more herbs in increments as they are mashed; the salt provides a bit of grit to mash with. Continue adding more herbs and slowly add more oil until you've used all of the herbs (you may not need all the oil). If using a food processor, simply add all the herbs, 1 tablespoon of salt, and the olive oil all at once and pulse to combine. The herb mixture should be a bit soupy, a little oily, and very fragrant. It may taste salty, but keep in mind that the fines herbes will season and perfume the beets and onions.

INGREDIENT NOTE: CANDY-STRIPED BEETS

Also known as *chioggia*, these beautiful scarlet red beets have interior rings of reddish pink and white. This specialty Italian variety is notable for its attractive color and relative absence of bleeding, making the halibut a picturesque and colorful dish.

Hanger steaks work well in this salad because they have so much flavor. Tossed with the romaine, blue cheese, a slightly garlicky oregano vinaigrette, and large crisp sourdough croutons, this is a very popular lunch entrée. Somewhat oversized, rustic sourdough croutons are the perfect addition to soup or salad. A snap to prepare, they are free-form and not cut into perfect cubes, which gives them a country look. To make rustic croutons, cut the crust from a day-old loaf of sourdough bread; with your fingers, pull off biggish, chunky pieces. Toss the bread with 2 tablespoons of olive oil and season with salt and pepper. Transfer to a preheated oven at 325°F and bake until the croutons emerge golden and crisp, about 10 minutes.

1 small onion, grated

2 tablespoons red wine vinegar

1 teaspoon freshly grated lemon zest

2 teaspoons ground coriander

1 teaspoon ground allspice

Pinch of freshly ground black pepper

1 whole hanger steak (about 1½ pounds), trimmed and cut into 4 pieces

Kosher salt

1 tablespoon canola oil

12 ounces romaine lettuce, preferably red, whole leaves, rinsed and dried

2 cups large sourdough croutons

¾ cup Stilton, or other good blue cheese, crumbled into large pieces

¼ cup Oregano Vinaigrette (recipe follows)

To make the marinade for the steak, combine in a large container the grated onion, vinegar, lemon zest, coriander, allspice, and black pepper. Coat the hanger steak in the marinade and marinate for 1 to 2 hours at room temperature. Brush off as much of the marinade as you can before cooking the steaks and season them well with salt.

Heat a grill pan or cast-iron skillet over medium flame; don't turn it up too high or the outside of the beef will burn before the inside is cooked. Film the pan with oil and when it gets hazy, lay the steak in the pan. Grill the pieces of steak, turning with tongs from time to time, to sear well on all sides; this takes about 12 minutes total. The meat should still be medium-rare.

Remove the steaks to a cutting board, cover to keep warm, and let rest for 5 minutes to allow the juices to recirculate. Using a sharp knife, cut the steaks on a slight angle into ¼-inch slices.

To serve, put the lettuce leaves, croutons, and Stilton in a mixing bowl. Add the sliced steak and any juices collected on the board; season with salt and pepper. Drizzle with ¼ cup of the oregano vinaigrette, tossing with your hands to dress the salad lightly and evenly. Divide the salad equally among 4 large plates.

oregano vinaigrette

MAKES ABOUT ½ CUP

2 teaspoons freshly squeezed lemon juice

1 tablespoon red wine vinegar

1 garlic clove, minced

1 tablespoon finely chopped fresh oregano

Kosher salt and freshly ground black pepper

½ cup extra-virgin olive oil

In a mixing bowl, combine the lemon juice, vinegar, garlic, and oregano; season lightly with salt and pepper. Whisk to blend and dissolve the salt. Slowly add the oil in a stream while whisking to emulsify; reserve at room temperature until needed. Keep any leftover vinaigrette covered in the refrigerator for up to 3 days.

LOBSTER SALAD WITH FENNEL, ARUGULA, AND YOGURT VINAIGRETTE SERVES 4

The yogurt vinaigrette doubles as a creamy marinade for Greek-style lamb. Whatever you do, refrain from using non- and lowfat yogurt, which don't possess the creamy richness needed for the dish; . . . diet tomorrow. If you cannot find Greek-style yogurt in your area, buy good-quality whole-milk yogurt and let it drain in the refrigerator overnight (either in cheesecloth or a fine-mesh strainer). The drained yogurt will then approximate the consistency of the Greek yogurt. All of the ingredients for the salad can be prepared ahead of time. Then, assembling the salad becomes a quick affair.

4 live lobsters (1 1/2 pounds each)
1 tablespoon sea salt
1/2 fennel bulb, trimmed, halved, and
    very thinly sliced
12 assorted cherry tomatoes, halved
1 cup baby arugula, rinsed and dried
Kosher salt and freshly ground black pepper
Juice of 1/2 lemon
1/4 cup extra-virgin olive oil
1 cup Yogurt Vinaigrette (recipe follows)
Chopped fresh chives, for garnish

To cook the lobsters, fill a large stockpot three-quarters of the way with water and add the sea salt; bring to a rapid boil over medium-high heat. Carefully ease 2 of the lobsters into the boiling water, and cook for 8 minutes, until the shells are bright red. Using tongs, carefully remove the lobsters from the pot and put them on a large platter. Bring the pot of salt water back up to a boil and repeat with the remaining 2 lobsters.

Working with rubber gloves, use a sort of sideways twist to break the legs, claws, and tails off of the bodies. Using a big sharp knife, break off the shells and split the tails in half lengthwise. If there are any visible veins or roe along the top of the tail, gently wash them away with cold water. Set aside the tails. Place the knuckles and claws on the work surface, whack them open, remove the shell, and carefully remove the meat with your fingers. Try to keep the claw meat in one piece.

Fill a mixing bowl with ice water and soak the fennel slices in it for about 15 minutes to crisp them up. Put the fennel in a salad spinner or pat with paper towels to dry well.

In a mixing bowl, toss together the lobster knuckles, fennel, tomatoes, and arugula; season with salt and pepper. Make a quick dressing by combining the juice of 1/2 lemon with the olive oil in a small bowl, whisking to blend; season with salt and pepper. Drizzle the lemon dressing on the lobster salad; toss to moisten.

To serve, pool 1/4 cup of the yogurt vinaigrette onto each of 4 plates and put a big handful of salad next to the vinaigrette circle. Lay half a lobster tail at 8 o'clock and the other at 4 o'clock. Nestle a claw in each tail half and then shower with chopped chives.

yogurt vinaigrette
MAKES ABOUT 1 1/4 CUPS
Juice of 1/2 lemon
1 garlic clove, finely grated
Kosher salt and freshly ground black pepper
3/4 cup extra-virgin olive oil
1/2 cup Greek-style or regular whole-milk yogurt
    strained overnight in cheesecloth

To make the yogurt vinaigrette, whisk together the lemon juice, garlic, and a generous pinch of salt and pepper. Slowly add the oil in a stream while whisking to emulsify the vinaigrette. Whisk in the yogurt until well blended and without lumps. Reserve at room temperature until needed. Keep any leftover vinaigrette covered in the refrigerator for up to 3 days.

Monkfish is often referred to as *anglerfish* in Europe. They are meaty bottom-dwelling fish that have a dense texture and sweet meat, similar to lobster (in fact, the fish has been called "poor man's lobster"). The robust porcini wine sauce is a natural accompaniment to grilled steak as well as fish.

If you make the sausage and lentils the night before, this elegant and easy dish is a quick one to put together.

1 cotechino sausage or kielbasa (about 8 ounces; see Ingredient Note)
5 fresh thyme sprigs
2 bay leaves
2 cups dry white wine, such as Pinot Grigio
1 cup dried French green lentils
Bouquet garni (6 parsley stems, 4 celery leaves, 2 thyme sprigs, and 1 bay leaf tied together with kitchen string)
Kosher salt and freshly ground black pepper
5 tablespoons extra-virgin olive oil
1 carrot, finely diced
1 celery stalk, finely diced
½ onion, finely diced
4 monkfish fillets (6 ounces each), cleaned
Porcini Red Wine Sauce (recipe follows)

Prick the cotechino in several places with a fork. Put the sausage in a large saucepan with the thyme and bay leaves. Cover the ingredients with the wine and 2 cups of water. Bring to a boil, then reduce the heat to low. Place a saucer on top of the sausage to weigh it down so it stays submerged in the liquid. Simmer for 45 minutes. Cool the cotechino in the broth.

Set aside the sausage and strain the cotechino poaching liquid into another pot to remove the herbs. Add the lentils and bouquet garni to the poaching liquid and simmer, uncovered, on low heat for 20 to 30 minutes, until the lentils are soft but not falling apart; remove the bouquet garni and season with salt and pepper. There should still be about ½ cup of broth left in the pot. The sausage and lentils may be prepared a day ahead. If so, wrap the sausage in plastic so it doesn't dry out and chill the lentils. Bring both back to room temperature before proceeding with the recipe.

To prepare the sautéed aromatic vegetables for the lentils, coat a sauté pan with 2 tablespoons of olive oil and add the finely diced carrot, celery, and onion; season with salt and pepper. Sauté for 5 to 10 minutes, just until tender but not brown. Combine the lentils and the aromatic vegetable garnish and mix well. Use any liquid left from the lentils to moisten the mixture. Cover and hold warm.

Preheat the oven to 400°F.

Line a sheet pan with foil and brush it with 1 tablespoon of oil. Cut the sausage into 12 slices and lay the slices on the prepared sheet pan in a single layer. Bake for 5 minutes, until hot and sizzling.

Cut the monkfish into medallions, about 2 ounces each, and season well with salt and pepper. Place a large nonstick pan over high heat and coat with the remaining 2 tablespoons of oil. Lay the monkfish medallions in the pan, without crowding. Sear for 3 minutes, without moving the medallions around. When the undersides of the fish look caramelized, turn them over and sear the other side for another 2 minutes.

To serve, arrange 3 slices of sausage in the center of each plate (at 12, 4, and 8 o'clock on the plate). In the center of the triangle, spoon a quarter of the lentils, lay the monkfish medallions on the lentils, and spoon some of the porcinis on top. Drizzle a couple of tablespoons of the red wine sauce all around.

porcini red wine sauce

2 ounces dried porcini mushrooms, wiped of grit

2 tablespoons extra-virgin olive oil

1 large shallot, finely chopped

Kosher salt and freshly ground black pepper

1 cup dry red wine, such as Cabernet Sauvignon or Syrah

2 cups Brown Veal Stock (page 230) or Chicken Stock (page 233)

To rehydrate the porcinis, place the mushrooms in a small bowl with ¾ cup of boiling water. Let the mushrooms steep for 20 minutes, until they are very soft. Remove the porcinis from the liquid, coarsely chop, and set aside. Strain the mushroom liquid through a fine-mesh sieve or coffee filter to remove any residual sand; reserve.

Place a sauté pan over medium heat and coat with the oil. When the oil is hot, add the chopped shallot and sauté for 3 to 5 minutes, until soft. Fold in the porcinis and season with salt and pepper. Cook for a couple of minutes to combine and then add the reserved porcini liquid. Cook the liquid down to a syrup, until it is almost all evaporated. Pour in the wine and simmer for 5 to 10 minutes, until reduced by three-quarters and only about ¼ cup remains. Pour in the stock and continue to simmer until the sauce is thick and has reduced by half, to about 1 cup; season with salt and pepper. Add a splash of red wine at the end to brighten up the flavor if desired. Cover and keep warm.

INGREDIENT NOTE: COTECHINO SAUSAGE

A cotechino is a large, rather gelatinous pork sausage with links about 3 inches in diameter and 8 inches long. The meat is commonly seasoned with clove, nutmeg, and garlic, giving the sausage a wintry essence. The cotechino-lentil pairing is one of the most classic marriages in Italian cooking; traditionally the duo is served on New Year's Eve to bring good fortune and luck.

COLORADO RACK OF LAMB WITH STUFFED PIQUILLO PEPPERS SERVES 4

Although the influences for this dish are a little all over the map—piquillo peppers (Spain), the braised lamb stuffing (Morocco), the fava and mint salad (Italy)—the end result is delicious! If your butcher cannot get Colorado lamb, Australian and New Zealand racks of lamb are also very good. Ask your butcher for a rack of rib chops (not loin chops) for this recipe. The braised lamb for the peppers can be done a day or two in advance. The mild red Spanish pepper, the piquillo, is the perfect size for stuffing; triangular in shape, they have a uniquely curved point (piquillo). The stuffed peppers can be made ahead and reheated before serving. La Kama, a fragrant spice mix, has a Moroccan influence and works well rubbed on roasted chicken.

1 whole rack of lamb, excess fat trimmed
    and bones frenched
2 fresh rosemary sprigs, hand torn
3 fresh thyme sprigs, hand torn
2 bay leaves
3 garlic cloves, smashed
3 tablespoons extra-virgin olive oil
Generous pinch of kosher salt and freshly
    ground black pepper
Fava, Pecorino, and Mint Salad (page 165)
Stuffed Piquillo Peppers (recipe follows)
Fleur de sel

Marinate the lamb rack with the rosemary, thyme, bay leaves, garlic, and oil, covered, in the refrigerator for as long as you have time to do so—at least 1 hour or up to overnight.

Preheat the oven to 475°F.

Pick the herbs and garlic off the lamb so they won't burn in the oven and season the meat well with salt and pepper. Place the lamb on a rack in a roasting pan with the ribs curving down. Roast in the oven for 15 to 20 minutes. Allow the rack of lamb to rest for 10 minutes, then slice into 8 double-chop pieces.

To serve, divide the fava, pecorino, and mint salad among 4 plates. Stand 2 lamb chops on each plate, bone up, and lay 2 hot stuffed piquillo peppers side by side. Season the lamb with fleur de sel.

stuffed piquillo peppers

MAKES 8 PEPPERS (SERVES 4)

2 lamb shanks (about 1 pound each)

Kosher salt and freshly ground black pepper

3 tablespoons canola oil

3 large Spanish onions, thinly sliced

6 garlic cloves, smashed

2 tablespoons La Kama Spice Mix
  (recipe follows)

2 quarts Brown Veal Stock (page 230)

1 cup dried apricots, cut in 1/2-inch dice

Juice of 1/2 lemon, or as needed

8 canned piquillo peppers

Preheat the oven to 350°F.

Season the lamb shanks well on all sides with salt and pepper. Place a large Dutch oven or other heavy-bottomed oven-safe pot over medium-high heat and add the oil. When the oil gets hazy, sear the lamb shanks, turning carefully with tongs, so all sides take on a brown caramel color; total cooking time will be about 10 minutes. Remove the shanks to a side plate. Add the onions and garlic to the drippings in the pot and cook, stirring with a wooden spoon, for about 10 to 15 minutes, until the onions have softened and begun to caramelize. Sprinkle with the kama spice and pour in the veal stock; bring to a boil, skimming any impurities that rise to the surface.

Nestle the shanks back into the pot; there should be enough liquid to just cover them; add some water if needed. Cover the pot tightly and put it in the oven; braise the lamb

shanks for 2 1/2 hours, until almost falling off the bone.

Using tongs, transfer the lamb shanks to a large platter and allow to cool slightly. When cool enough to handle, pull off the meat from the bones, tearing it into bite-size pieces and putting them into a large bowl. Strain the braising liquid and reserve it for another use (I recommend using this stock to cook white beans or as a soup base).

Put the braised onions and garlic in the bowl with the lamb and add the dried apricots. Mix the lamb stuffing with a large wooden spoon to combine, taking care not to break up the meat too much. Taste for seasoning, adding salt, pepper, a little more kama spice, and a bit of lemon juice, if necessary.

Cool the lamb filling to room temperature before stuffing the piquillo peppers. Use a teaspoon to fill the peppers, and be careful not to overstuff or they may tear and burst open. Serve the stuffed piquillo peppers warm.

la kama spice mix

MAKES ABOUT 1/4 CUP

1 tablespoon ground ginger

1 tablespoon freshly ground black pepper

1 tablespoon turmeric

1/2 tablespoon ground cinnamon

1 teaspoon freshly grated nutmeg

To make the spice mix, combine all the dried spices in a small bowl and toss thoroughly to distribute well.

This is an unusual and unusually flavorful vegetarian risotto. Cooking the rice with red wine gives the finished risotto a beautiful deep brick red color. The sweetness of the butternut squash is a wonderful foil to the slight acidity of the red-wine-cooked risotto.

Amaretti cookies are light, airy Italian almond macaroons. The amaretti and orange gremolata provides additional textural and flavor elements that bring the dish together. It gets too moist if made way ahead of time, so put it together just before starting the risotto. This idea was a riff on the traditional squash ravioli filling—roasted pumpkin or squash, crushed amaretti cookies, and orange zest.

1 large butternut squash (about 2 pounds)
¼ cup extra-virgin olive oil
Kosher salt and freshly ground black pepper
3 cups Vegetable Stock (page 228)
1½ cups Italian red wine, such as Barolo or Chianti
¼ cup (½ stick) unsalted butter
3 shallots, finely chopped
1 cup Arborio rice
½ cup coarsely grated Parmigiano-Reggiano
Amaretti and Orange Gremolata (recipe follows)

Preheat the oven to 375°F.

The butternut squash is vaguely pear shaped—wide at the bottom and skinnier at the top. For this recipe, we use only the narrow neck of the squash; the skin tends to be softer and there aren't any seeds and stringy membranes to deal with. (Save the big part of the squash for another use.) Using a heavy chef's knife or a cleaver, cut off the squash's neck, right about where the bulbous bottom meets it. With a vegetable peeler or paring knife, peel off the skin to expose the orange flesh. Cut the squash into ½-inch cubes and put in a small mixing bowl; you should have 1 cup.

Toss the squash cubes with 2 tablespoons of the oil to coat well; season generously with salt and pepper. Spread the squash on a foil-lined sheet pan and roast for 10 to 12 minutes, rotating the pan halfway through baking so it cooks evenly. The butternut squash should look caramelized and golden on the surface and tender when pierced with a knife. As an alternative, sauté the cubes of squash in olive oil in a large pan over medium heat, for about 8 minutes, until cooked through and golden. Put the roasted squash on a side plate to cool.

Combine the vegetable stock and 1 cup of wine in a saucepan over medium-low heat; keep it warm at a low simmer, but don't let the liquid boil.

Place a large sauté pan over high heat and add the remaining 2 tablespoons of oil and 2 tablespoons of butter. When the butter is melted, add the shallots and cook and stir for 3 minutes, until translucent. Add the rice, and stir for a minute or two, until the grains are opaque and slightly toasted; season with salt and pepper.

Deglaze with the remaining ½ cup of wine, which will bubble up for a minute, and cook until it's almost totally evaporated, about 2 minutes. Pour in 1 cup of the warm stock/wine mixture. Stir with a wooden spoon, until the rice has absorbed all the liquid, and then add another cup. Keep stirring while adding the stock mixture 1 cup at a time, allowing the rice to drink it in before adding more. The rice will look beautiful—a vibrant purplish red color.

After about 15 minutes, when there's about 1 cup left of the stock/wine mixture, fold in the roasted butternut squash. Add the last dose of liquid; cook and stir an additional 3 to 5 minutes to incorporate the squash and heat through. Taste the risotto. It should be al dente—definitely not mushy but not raw either.

Mix the remaining 2 tablespoons of butter into the hot risotto and top with a fresh grating of Parmesan. Finish the dish with a shower of the amaretti gremolata and serve.

amaretti and orange gremolata
1 small orange
¼ cup chopped fresh flat-leaf parsley
2 tablespoons well-crushed amaretti cookies

Using a vegetable peeler or sharp paring knife, slice off a nice fat strip of orange peel, avoiding the bitter white pith. Finely chop the zest into tiny, tiny pieces, about 2 teaspoons worth. Although it may seem faster to simply use a microplane or other zester, I find that for this recipe, too much oil comes out of the rind, making the gremolata clumpy and kind of wet. It's worth the extra minute to chop the peel by hand.

Put the chopped orange zest in a small bowl; add the parsley and crushed cookie crumbs. Toss the mixture gently but evenly. Reserve the amaretti gremolata at room temperature to garnish the risotto.

When local white and bicolor corn become available in New York, this is one way for us to showcase it. Succulent lobster meat, freshly shucked peas, and lots of sweet corn combine to make a really wonderful summer risotto. If you can't find savory and don't want to use thyme, you could substitute fresh basil. Traditionally, risottos containing seafood do not include cheese, but feel free to add a little freshly grated Parmigiano if you like.

1 tablespoon sea salt

1 live lobster (1½ pounds)

4 cups Vegetable Stock (page 228)

5 tablespoons unsalted butter

2 large shallots, minced

1 cup Arborio rice

Generous pinch of kosher salt and freshly ground black pepper

½ cup dry white wine, such as Sauvignon Blanc

2 ears sweet white corn, shucked, kernels cut from the cob (about 1 cup)

1 cup sweet peas, frozen or fresh (if using fresh peas, blanch for 2 minutes in salted boiling water; if using frozen, run under cool water for 2 minutes to thaw)

1 teaspoon chopped fresh savory or thyme leaves

Juice of ¼ lemon, if desired

Fill a large stockpot three-quarters of the way with water and add the sea salt; bring to a rapid boil over medium-high heat. Carefully ease the lobster into the pot, and cook for 8 minutes, until the shell is bright red. Using tongs, carefully remove the lobster to a side platter.

Working with rubber gloves, use a sort of sideways twist to break the legs, claws, and tails off of the bodies. Using a big knife, split the tails in half lengthwise. Gently wash away any visible veins or roe with cold water. On a work surface, rest the tails on their sides and, using the palm of your hand, press down on them to break off the outer shells; cut the tail meat into bite-size pieces. With the back of a knife, crack the claws and wiggle the meat out from the shell. Place the knuckles on the work surface, whack them open, remove the shell, and carefully pick out the meat with your fingers. You should have at least 1 cup of meat.

Heat the stock in a saucepan over medium-low flame; keep warm at a simmer, but don't let it boil.

Place a large sauté pan over high heat and add 3 tablespoons of butter. When the butter is melted, add the shallots and cook them for 3 minutes, until translucent, stirring often. Add the rice, and stir for a minute or two, until the grains are opaque and slightly toasted; season with salt and pepper.

Deglaze with the wine and cook until almost evaporated. Pour in 1 cup of the warm stock, stir until the rice has absorbed all the liquid, and then add another cup. Keep stirring while adding the stock 1 cup at a time, allowing the rice to drink it in before adding more, until the rice has been cooking for about 12 minutes.

Fold in the corn and cook for 1 minute to incorporate. Add the peas and savory, cook another minute or two, until the rice is almost tender. Taste the rice frequently at this point, keeping in mind that it will continue to cook even after you turn off the flame—it should not be dry or mushy.

Fold in the lobster, adjust the seasoning, give a squeeze of lemon juice if you like, and finish the risotto with the remaining 2 tablespoons of butter. Serve immediately in warm bowls.

PAN-ROASTED POUSSIN WITH TARRAGON JUS, WILD MUSHROOMS, AND SNAP PEAS

Poussin is French for a "very young, small chicken," usually only a month or two old. They are the perfect size for a single serving and cook very quickly. In the market, a poussin is also referred to as a spring chicken. If poussin are not available, cornish game hens work as a fine substitute. Have a butcher butterfly the poussin (or spatchcock, as the English call it). To butterfly them yourself: place the poussin breast side down on a chopping board. Cut along either side of the backbone with poultry shears or a sharp pair of kitchen scissors and lift out the bone. Turn over the poussin, open it up, and press down firmly along the breastbone until it lies flat like a book. Be sure to reserve the bones and giblets.

6 tablespoons canola oil

4 poussin (1 pound each), butterflied, backbone removed and chopped, neck, gizzards, and heart reserved

3 shallots, coarsely chopped

1 carrot, coarsely chopped

3 garlic cloves, coarsely chopped

½ teaspoon whole black peppercorns

½ cup dry white wine, such as Sauvignon Blanc

3 cups Chicken Stock (page 233)

3 fresh tarragon sprigs

Kosher salt and freshly ground black pepper

½ pound sugar snap peas, ends trimmed and strings removed

3 tablespoons unsalted butter

½ pound assorted wild mushrooms, such as chanterelles, oysters, and shiitakes, wiped of grit

1 shallot, finely diced

1 bunch scallions, white and green parts, cut into 1-inch pieces

1 fresh tarragon sprig, leaves stripped from the stem and finely chopped

To make the jus, put a stockpot over medium-high heat and coat with 2 tablespoons of the oil. When the oil gets hazy, add the poussin bones and giblets. Cook, stirring constantly, for about 5 to 8 minutes, until browned.

Add the chopped shallots, carrot, garlic, and peppercorns. Continue cooking and stirring for 5 to 10 minutes; the poussin bones and giblets should be brown, the vegetables soft, and the pot should have nice caramelized bits on the bottom. Deglaze with the white wine, scraping with a wooden spoon to pull up the flavors. Reduce the wine completely to cook out the alcohol. Add the chicken stock. Bring to a boil, reduce to a simmer, skimming any impurities that rise to the surface. Simmer gently until the jus has a good flavor and is reduced by at least half, about 15 to 20 minutes.

Strain the jus through a fine strainer into another small pot, pressing with the back of a wooden spoon to extract as much flavor as possible from the aromatics. Bring the sauce to a boil, and then reduce to low. Simmer gently, skimming any remaining fat from the surface. Turn off the heat, add the tarragon sprigs, and let stand for 10 minutes to infuse the flavor. Pull the tarragon out with tongs and keep the sauce warm.

Season the poussin on both sides with a generous amount of salt and pepper; you should be able to see the seasoning. Heat 2 large sauté pans over medium-high heat. Add 2 tablespoons of the remaining canola oil to each pan. Alternatively, you may cook the poussin in batches if you don't have several large pans. Lay 2 poussin in each pan, skin side down, and cook until the skin is crispy, 10 to 15 minutes. Carefully flip over the poussin and continue to cook for 3 more minutes, until fully cooked. Remove the poussin from the pans and reserve warm.

Meanwhile, to blanch the snap peas, bring a large pot of lightly salted water to a boil. Boil the snap peas for 1 minute; they become tender very quickly. Drain them and plunge in an ice bath to "shock" them, i.e., to stop the cooking process and cool them down right away. This procedure also sets their vibrant color. Drain the snap peas in a colander and reserve.

Place a clean medium sauté pan over high heat. Add the butter and just before it begins to brown, add the mushrooms. Season well with salt and pepper. Cook, stirring occasionally, until the mushroom liquid evaporates and they begin to brown, about 6 minutes. When the mushrooms are caramelized, stir in the diced shallot and scallions and continue to sauté until soft, just another minute. Fold in the blanched snap peas and toss for 2 to 3 minutes to incorporate and heat through. Adjust the seasoning and finish with a shower of chopped tarragon.

To serve, divide the vegetables among 4 plates, place the poussin skin side up on the vegetables, and spoon a few tablespoons of the tarragon jus around the crispy birds.

This recipe is all about ingredients—high-quality veal and very fresh wild mushrooms. Top-quality mushrooms will not hide inferior meat and shriveled mushrooms won't do a great veal chop justice. Shop with care and get the best veal chops you can afford. If chanterelles are too expensive or just look old, buy whatever wild mushrooms look and smell best. Tying the veal chops around the side is not imperative but results in a better presentation. The string holds the shape of the chop and ensures even cooking. Serve with Grilled Broccoli Raab with Garlic-Chili Oil as a side. Any leftover sauce may be frozen for up to three months and used to top steak or chicken.

5 tablespoons extra-virgin olive oil
1 shallot, minced
4 garlic cloves, smashed
2 tablespoons fresh rosemary needles
1 whole star anise
1/2 teaspoon cracked black pepper
3 bay leaves
1 tablespoon balsamic vinegar
1/2 cup dry white wine, such as Sauvignon Blanc
4 large veal rib chops (12 ounces each), frenched and tied preferably
2 tablespoons unsalted butter
2 fresh thyme sprigs, plus more for garnish
Grilled Broccoli Raab with Garlic-Chili Oil (page 168)
1 1/2 cups Chanterelle and Madeira Sauce (recipe follows)

To make the marinade for the veal chops, coat a saucepan with 3 tablespoons of the oil and place over medium-low heat. Add the shallot, garlic, and rosemary; sauté for 5 minutes, until fragrant. Add the star anise, pepper, bay leaves, vinegar, and wine. Raise the heat to medium and bring the marinade to a quick boil. Cool to room temperature and pour the marinade over the veal chops. Cover and refrigerate for at least 2 hours or up to overnight.

Heat a large sauté pan over high flame and film with the remaining 2 tablespoons of oil. When the oil gets hazy, carefully add the chops (you may have to do this in batches if your pan cannot comfortably fit all 4 chops). Sear the veal chops for 5 to 7 minutes on one side without moving them to ensure the formation of a nice crust. Turn over the chops and continue to cook for another 6 to 8 minutes. For the last 2 to 3 minutes of cooking, add the butter to the pan, and, when it foams, carefully add the thyme (the moisture in the herb coming in contact with the hot fat will cause a lot of snap, crackle, and pop!). Tilt the pan and use a spoon to baste the chops with thyme butter. At this point the veal chops should be cooked through. Remove them to a side plate and let them rest for 5 minutes.

To serve, lay 4 or 5 pieces of broccoli raab toward the top of 4 plates, lean a veal chop against the broccoli raab, and spoon the chanterelle and Madeira sauce on the meat. Garnish each veal chop with a thyme sprig.

chanterelle and madeira sauce

MAKES 1 1/2 TO 2 CUPS

2 tablespoons unsalted butter

1/2 pound chanterelle mushrooms, wiped of
   grit, halved or quartered if large

Kosher salt and freshly ground black pepper

2 large shallots, minced

1 tablespoon fresh thyme leaves

1/2 cup Madeira

1 quart Brown Veal Stock (page 230)

Place a sauté pan over high heat. Add the butter and, just before it begins to brown, add the chanterelles. Season well with salt and pepper. Cook, stirring occasionally, until the mushroom liquid evaporates and the mushrooms begin to brown, about 6 minutes. When they are caramelized, stir in the shallots and thyme. Continue to sauté until soft, about 5 minutes.

Deglaze with the Madeira and cook down the wine completely. Pour in the veal stock and continue to simmer, lowering the heat to medium, until the sauce is thick and has reduced by half, to about 2 cups; season with salt and pepper. Add a splash of Madeira at the end to brighten up the flavor if desired. Cover and keep warm. The sauce may be made in advance and kept covered in the refrigerator for 3 or 4 days. Reheat before serving.

ROAST LEG OF LAMB SANDWICH SERVES 4

This boneless stuffed leg of lamb is wonderful as a main course on its own, but at Lever House we go the extra mile to create a stellar sandwich that makes lunch an event. The inspiration for this very tasty sandwich came from a leg of lamb I cooked at my mother's house one weekend. As usual, I forgot that I wasn't cooking in a restaurant for a lot of people and made too much food. The lamb sandwich was the happy solution to the leftover problem. I hope you enjoy it as much as my family did and as much as our guests have.

¾ cup pitted oil-cured black olives, preferably Moroccan
¼ cup fresh rosemary needles
1 garlic clove, smashed
¼ teaspoon red pepper flakes
2 heaping teaspoons juniper berries, smashed
2 anchovy fillets
3 tablespoons extra-virgin olive oil
1 butterflied leg of lamb (about 4 pounds)
Kosher salt and freshly ground black pepper
4 squares thick focaccia bread (about 4 × 4 inches)
½ cup Spicy Eggplant (page 181)
½ cup Artichoke Tapenade (recipe follows)

To prepare the lamb stuffing, put the olives, rosemary, garlic, red pepper flakes, juniper berries, and anchovies in a food processor; pulse to achieve a coarse mixture. Add 2 tablespoons of the oil and pulse a couple more times to incorporate.

Lay the piece of lamb on a work surface, open it up like a book, and trim any excess fat. Generously season the inside of the lamb with salt and pepper. Smear the stuffing down the length of the lamb and roll the meat lengthwise over the stuffing, tucking in the ends to hold the filling inside. Tie the roast with butcher's twine in 1-inch intervals. Season the lamb roll on all sides with a generous amount of salt and pepper; you should see the seasoning on the meat. If you have time, let the lamb sit for 1 hour to marinate.

Preheat the oven to 475°F.

Brush the lamb roast with the remaining tablespoon of oil and lay the lamb in a rack set in a roasting pan.

Cook the stuffed lamb for 15 minutes. Reduce the oven temperature to 375°F, and continue to roast for 30 to 40 additional minutes. The meat should be pink in the center and the internal temperature should read 125°F when tested with a meat thermometer. Allow the lamb to stand for 10 minutes to let the juices settle; the internal temperature will rise about 10 degrees. Remove the string and slice the lamb roll into ¼-inch rounds. For this dish, you will need only 12 slices, 3 per person. When completely cool, wrap the leftover lamb roll in plastic and slice as needed—it's even good for snacking.

To serve, halve the focaccia squares horizontally. Lightly toast the bread if desired. Spread the spicy eggplant evenly on the cut side of the bottom halves of the bread. Shingle 3 pieces of the stuffed lamb on the eggplant; spread the artichoke tapenade on the cut side of the focaccia tops, put the sandwiches together, and press gently. Cut each sandwich diagonally in half. Serve at room temperature or cold.

artichoke tapenade

MAKES 1 CUP

2 fresh artichokes

1 lemon plus 2 tablespoons freshly squeezed
lemon juice

1 hard-boiled egg

2 tablespoons capers, drained, rinsed, and
patted dry

1 anchovy fillet

¾ cup freshly grated pecorino

¼ cup extra-virgin olive oil

Kosher salt and freshly ground black pepper

To clean the artichokes down to the bottom or heart, rotate the artichoke as you trim off all the outer leaves with a sharp paring knife. Cut off the stems, inner leaves, and any green from the base. Remove the inner beard with a spoon or melon baller. Squeeze the lemon into a bowl of water and put the artichoke heart in it to prevent it from discoloring while you clean and cut the second choke.

Coarsely chop the artichoke hearts and put them in a food processor. Add the hard-boiled egg, capers, anchovy fillet, and lemon juice; pulse to coarsely chop. Add the cheese and pulse briefly to combine. Pour in the olive oil in 3 additions, pulsing in short bursts in between to incorporate; the tapenade should still be chunky. Taste for salt and pepper, adjusting as necessary. If you have time, make this ahead of time to let the flavors marry. The Tuscan-inspired artichoke tapenade is ideal to spread on toasted Italian bread or on a grilled cheese sandwich.

SLOW-ROASTED SALMON SALAD WITH LEMON CREAM DRESSING SERVES 4

This is a popular and relatively light lunch entrée from our menu. In season, we try to use as many different beans as we can find at the greenmarket for this salad. If you can't find yellow wax beans, just double up on the haricots verts. When cooking the salmon, please be aware that slow-roasted salmon will look almost raw, even when it is cooked. Also, when you make the lemon cream, whisk the dressing only enough to mix the ingredients. Too much aeration can curdle the cream.

1 English cucumber, peeled, seeded, and
    sliced in ⅛-inch-thick half moons
1 tablespoon kosher salt, plus additional to
    taste
¼ pound haricots verts or thin green beans,
    stems trimmed
¼ pound yellow wax beans, stems trimmed
4 salmon fillets (6 ounces each), skin
    removed
3 tablespoons canola oil
Freshly ground black pepper
2 small heads of butter lettuce, such as
    Boston or Bibb, hand torn
1 tablespoon chopped fresh chives, plus
    more for garnish
1 teaspoon chopped fresh flat-leaf parsley
1 teaspoon chopped fresh tarragon
1 teaspoon chopped fresh chervil
Lemon Cream Dressing (recipe follows)

Place the sliced cucumbers in a colander and sprinkle with 1 tablespoon of salt, making sure that all the pieces are salted. Put the colander in the sink or over a bowl, and let sit for 30 minutes to drain. The salt will draw out the moisture. The cucumbers should be slightly limp but still crisp. Taste them and if they are too salty, rinse them under cool water and drain well. Reserve in the refrigerator.

To blanch the haricots verts and the wax beans, bring a large pot of lightly salted water to a boil. Boil the beans for only 2 minutes (do this in batches to keep the water at a rolling boil if necessary). Drain the beans and plunge in an ice bath to "shock" them, i.e., to stop the cooking process and cool them down right away. This procedure also sets the vibrant color of the green beans. Drain the blanched beans and reserve in the refrigerator.

Preheat the oven to 250°F.

Fill a small baking pan with hot water and put it on the bottom rack of the oven; this will create a moist environment for cooking the salmon.

Lightly brush the salmon fillets on both sides with 2 tablespoons of the oil and season with salt and pepper. Line a large baking pan with foil and brush it with the remaining tablespoon of oil to prevent sticking. Lay the salmon fillets in the prepared pan. The fillets should not touch each other, so air can circulate as the fish cooks. Bake the salmon for 10 minutes until medium-rare; the fish will still be pink and may look raw to the naked eye, but will be cooked inside. The texture definitely changes and firms up a bit; you should be able to cut the salmon with a spoon.

To serve, in a large bowl combine the cucumbers, blanched beans, lettuce, and chopped chives, parsley, tarragon, and chervil; season lightly with salt and pepper. Dress the salad with 3 to 4 tablespoons of the dressing and toss the ingredients gently using your hands to combine. Divide the salad among 4 plates, lay a warm salmon fillet on top of each portion, and garnish with chopped chives. Serve the remaining lemon cream on the side.

lemon cream dressing

MAKES ABOUT ½ CUP

Juice of ½ lemon (about 3 tablespoons)
Kosher salt and freshly ground black pepper
½ cup heavy cream

Squeeze the lemon juice into a stainless-steel bowl and add a pinch of salt and pepper. Slowly and gently whisk in the heavy cream until just combined. Do not overwhip the cream or it will become grainy. Chill before serving. This lemon cream may be made a few hours in advance and is also a flavorful dip for blanched vegetables.

Skate is a wonderful fish, inexpensive yet full of flavor. Although it looks unwieldy whole, your fishmonger should be able to skin and fillet it for you. In any case, make sure that it has no odor. If there is even a hint of ammonia from it, the fish is over the hill and won't be good. Skate's meaty flavor can stand up to (and benefit from) an assertive sauce. The balsamic-mushroom vinaigrette we drizzle over the skate is a great example. The reduced mushroom essence and musky sweetness from the balsamic coupled with the exotic spice mix with which we season the skate make this dish memorable.

2 tablespoons Spice Mix (page 228)
4 filleted skate wings (5 to 7 ounces each; see Ingredient Note)
2 tablespoons unsalted butter
Roasted Mushrooms (page 179)
Fingerling Potatoes (page 180)
Kosher salt and freshly ground black pepper
2 tablespoons canola oil
1 cup Balsamic-Mushroom Vinaigrette (recipe follows)
Watercress, stems trimmed, for garnish

Sprinkle the fragrant spice mix on both sides of the skate wings.

Heat a large sauté pan over medium heat and add the butter. When the butter foams, toss in the roasted mushrooms, along with their liquid, and the fingerling potatoes. Sauté for 2 to 3 minutes to combine; season with a generous amount of salt and pepper. Cover to keep warm.

Heat a large sauté pan over medium heat and coat with the oil. When the oil gets hazy, lay the seasoned skate wings in the pan and sear for 2 minutes; do this in batches to avoid overcrowding the pan. Turn over the fish with a spatula and cook the other side for about 2 more minutes.

To serve, lay 1 skate wing on each of 4 plates. In the crescent of the fanned wing, spoon a small pile of the mushrooms and potatoes. Drizzle the skate and vegetables with about ¼ cup of the balsamic-mushroom vinaigrette and garnish with watercress.

balsamic-mushroom vinaigrette

MAKES ABOUT 1½ CUPS

¼ cup Mushroom Jus (page 233)
¼ cup good-quality balsamic vinegar, such as 12-year-old
6 cloves Roasted Garlic Confit (page 234)
Kosher salt and freshly ground black pepper
1 cup grapeseed oil

Combine in a blender the mushroom jus, vinegar, roasted garlic, and a generous pinch of salt and pepper. Puree at high speed until well mixed. With the motor running, slowly drizzle in the oil to emulsify; the vinaigrette will be fairly thick. Taste for seasoning, spoon the balsamic–mushroom vinaigrette into a plastic squeeze bottle for serving, and reserve at room temperature. Keep any leftover vinaigrette covered in the refrigerator for up to 3 days.

INGREDIENT NOTE: SKATE

For many years, the French have revered skate fish, serving it up simply with brown butter or lemon-caper sauce. Only recently has skate appeared on menus in fine dining restaurants in the States. For ease, ask your fish merchant to skin and fillet the skate for you; that's what he's there for.

MUSHROOM VINAIGRETTE SERVES 4

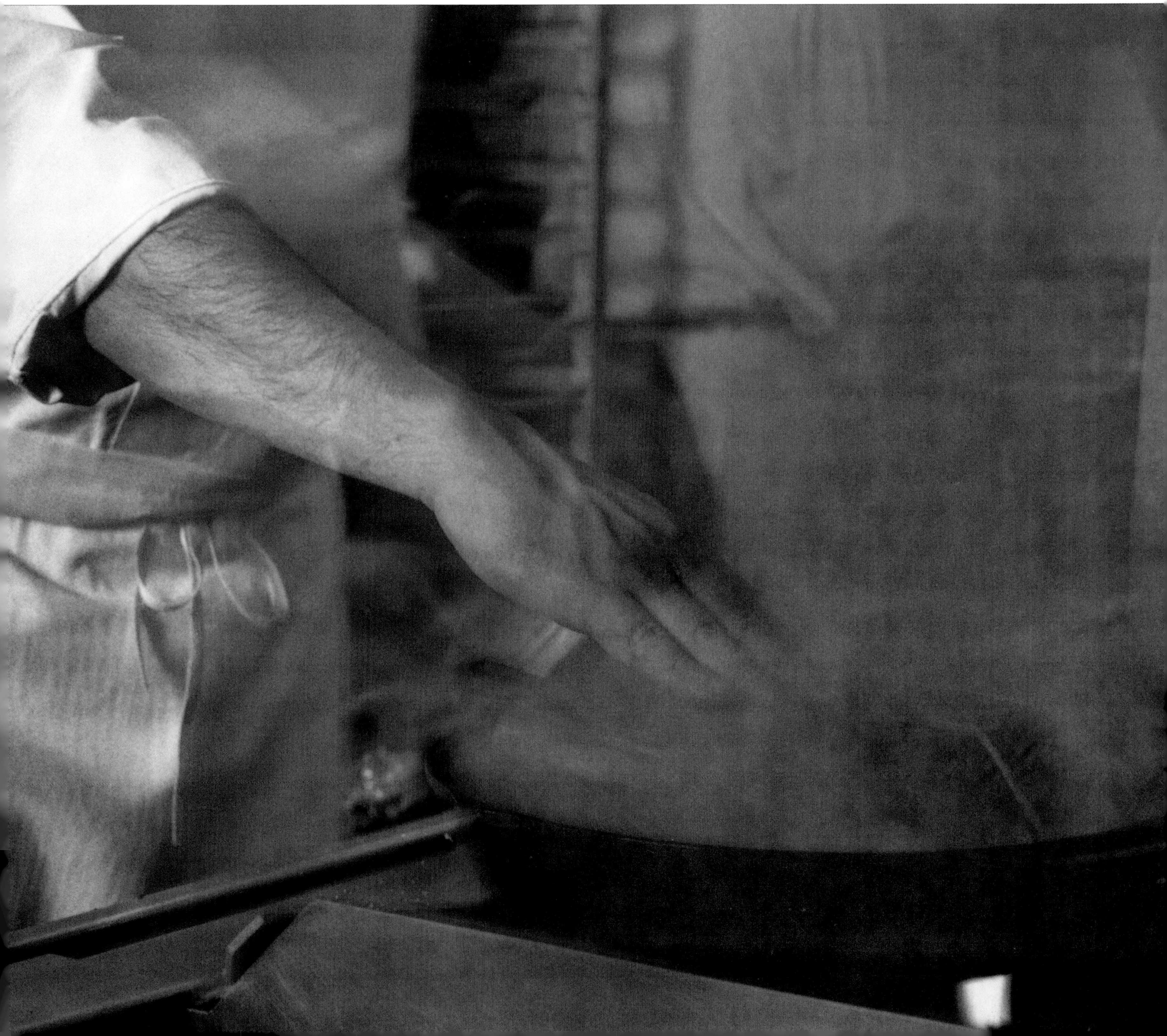

FROM THE GRILL

Grilling is a clean, quick, primal way to cook. Using direct heat virtually guarantees a slightly charred crust, and the beautiful grill marks make the foods look wonderful, too. A gas grill cannot be beat for convenience, although I am an ardent fan of the smoky flavor emitted from charcoal fires with wood chips. If it's too cold outside, a ridged (preferably cast-iron) grill pan on the stovetop will do the trick. You may also use the broiler, although this is easiest for steaks and chops.

Whatever apparatus you choose, always preheat your grill. If you can just barely hold your hand a few inches above the grill for a second or two, the temperature is about right. You don't want the exterior of the meat to brown before the inside is cooked through. Make sure the grill is clean. Very lightly oil both the grates and the food before you grill. Too much oil will flare up and smoke, giving the food an unpleasant, gassy flavor. When grilling fish and other fragile foods, try to move it as little as possible to minimize sticking and avoid the possibility of tearing. Steaks and chops are more forgiving; however, they usually take longer to grill and will need to be moved from a hot spot to a slightly cooler part of the grill to finish cooking.

ALASKAN BLACK COD WITH BABY BOK CHOY, CHARRED FENNEL, AND RED ONIONS

Black cod is actually not truly cod at all, but sablefish. To add to the confusion, in some markets, the white fish is also referred to as butterfish, dubbed so for its rich, creamy texture. Black cod is found all along the cold depths off the Pacific coast, and Alaskan is considered the best in quality for its tender, sweet flavor. A popular choice in Japanese restaurants and supermarkets, the fish is so heavily in demand in Japan that the vast majority of the Alaskan harvest is exported there. But in recent years, there's been a growing awareness of this supple finfish in the States; you're likely to see black cod featured on restaurant menus, perhaps redolent of miso and sake. In another preparation, you'll often find smoked black cod in New York delis; the fish's high fat content makes it an excellent choice for smoking. If you are landlocked and fresh sablefish/black cod is not available, check out the frozen section. The oily nature of the flesh stands up very well to freezing and makes a fine substitute for fresh.

2 heads baby bok choy
1 fennel bulb, halved, cored, sliced 1/4 to 1/2 inch thick
1 large red onion, halved and sliced 1/4 to 1/2 inch thick
Kosher salt and freshly ground black pepper
3 tablespoons extra-virgin olive oil, plus more for coating the fish
3 tablespoons unsalted butter
4 black cod fillets (about 6 ounces each), skin removed
1 teaspoon smoked Spanish paprika
1/2 cup Citrus Vinaigrette (page 137)

To blanch the bok choy, bring a large pot of lightly salted water to a boil. Cut the base off the bottoms of the stalks and pull off the cabbage stalks, leaving them whole. Boil the bok choy for only 1 minute; the leaves become tender very quickly. Drain the bok choy and plunge in an ice bath to "shock" them, i.e., to stop the cooking process and cool them down right away. Drain the blanched bok choy and dry well with paper towels. Set aside.

Put the sliced fennel and onion in a strainer and set in the sink or over a bowl; season generously with about 1 teaspoon of salt and ½ teaspoon of pepper and let sit for 30 minutes in order to draw the water out. Put the fennel and onion in a bowl and toss with 3 tablespoons of oil to coat.

Place a cast-iron skillet over medium-high heat. Add the fennel and onion to the hot pan; sauté quickly for 3 minutes to tenderize the vegetables and char slightly. The fennel and onion may be held hot or at room temperature.

To warm up the vegetables together, place a deep sauté pan over medium-low heat. Heat 2 tablespoons of water and then swirl in the butter. This duo is classically called a beurre monte, and will coat the vegetables. Just make sure the butter and water don't boil, as the two may separate—oil and water don't naturally mix, after all. Once the butter and water have become one and emulsified, add the blanched bok choy leaves and the stir-fried fennel and onion. Coat the vegetables in the butter sauce for a minute or 2 to combine and just warm through; season lightly with salt and pepper. Remove from the heat and cover to keep warm.

Rub the black cod fillets with oil and season both sides with paprika and a generous amount of salt and pepper. Place a large grill pan on 2 burners over medium-high heat or preheat an outdoor gas or charcoal grill and get it very hot. Lay the fish fillets on the hot grill, and sear for 2 to 3 minutes on each side, rotating halfway through cooking to "mark" them.

To serve, divide the vegetable mixture (bok choy, fennel, onion) among 4 plates using a slotted spoon or tongs. Lay a black cod fillet on top of the vegetables and spoon the citrus vinaigrette all around, letting the segments fall where they may.

citrus vinaigrette

MAKES ¾ TO 1 CUP

1 orange, seedless

1 lemon

1 lime

2 tablespoons minced shallots

1 sprig fresh lemon thyme, leaves stripped
   from the stem and finely chopped

¼ teaspoon coriander seed, coarsely ground

¼ teaspoon fennel seed, coarsely ground

1 teaspoon lavender honey

½ cup extra-virgin olive oil

Kosher salt and freshly ground black pepper

To segment the orange, lemon, and lime for the vinaigrette, first trim flat the top and bottom of each so it stands steady on a work surface; cut deep enough so you see the meat of the fruit. Using a paring knife, cut off the skin and bitter white pith of each piece of fruit, following the natural shape and turning the fruit as you do so. Trim off any white areas that remain. Hold each piece of fruit over a bowl to catch the citrus juices. Carefully cut along the membrane, on both sides of each segment to free the pieces, and let them drop into the bowl. Then squeeze the membrane over the wedges in the bowl to extract the remaining juice. Remove any seeds from the lemon.

Measure out 6 tablespoons of the fresh-squeezed citrus juices and put in a small mixing bowl. Add the shallots, thyme, coriander, fennel, and honey; whisk to combine. Slowly add the oil in a stream while whisking until the vinaigrette emulsifies. Taste and adjust seasoning.

Toss together the citrus segments (without any leftover collected juice in the bowl) and the vinaigrette just before serving.

GRILLED BLACK SEA BASS WITH CILANTRO-MINT SAUCE AND SAUTÉED SPINACH

The flavor of the grilled black sea bass with the cilantro-mint sauce is a powerful pairing. I don't usually cook with a lot of cilantro, but I was drawn to using it for this sauce in combination with mint and the almond milk because it works well with the meaty flavor of the fish and the slight char provided by the grill.

¼ cup Vegetable Stock (page 238),
    Fish Stock (page 232), or water
¼ cup Cilantro-Mint Sauce (recipe follows)
1 small orange
2 tablespoons extra-virgin olive oil,
    plus more for coating the fish
2 garlic cloves, smashed
1½ pounds fresh spinach, stems trimmed,
    washed well, and dried
Kosher salt and freshly ground black pepper
4 black sea bass fillets (about 6 ounces
    each), cleaned and scaled, skin on
    preferably

In a small pot over medium-low heat, bring the stock to a gentle simmer. Stir in the cilantro-mint sauce, and swirl gently to combine and heat through. Cover the sauce to keep warm over very low heat.

To make the sautéed spinach, using a vegetable peeler or sharp paring knife, slice off a nice fat strip of orange peel, avoiding the bitter white pith. Finely julienne the zest into tiny pieces, about 1 teaspoon worth.

Coat a large sauté pan with 2 tablespoons of oil and place over medium flame.

Add the garlic to flavor the oil and sauté for 2 minutes, until lightly golden but not brown and bitter; pull out the garlic and discard. Add the spinach in handfuls, folding the leaves over so they hit the bottom heat and wilt, adding more when there's room to; season with salt and pepper. Sprinkle with the orange zest and gently mix to incorporate.

Transfer the sautéed spinach to a colander and put it over the sink. Press gently with the back of a wooden spoon to squeeze out the excess water. Cover with a towel to keep warm.

Place a large grill pan on 2 burners over medium-high heat or preheat an outdoor gas or charcoal grill until very hot. Rub the sea bass fillets with oil and season both sides with a fair amount of salt and pepper. Lay the fish fillets on the hot grill, skin side down, and sear for about 3 minutes, rotating halfway through cooking to "mark" them and form a crust. Flip over the fish fillets and grill the flesh side for 2 more minutes.

To serve, divide the sautéed spinach among 4 plates, lay a black bass fillet on the spinach, skin side up, and spoon the warm cilantro-mint sauce around.

cilantro-mint sauce

MAKES 2 CUPS

1 cup fresh cilantro (about 2 bunches),
     washed, dried, and coarsely chopped

½ cup fresh mint, washed, dried, and
     coarsely chopped

14 garlic cloves, coarsely chopped

8 jalapeños, seeded and coarsely chopped

4 teaspoons ground cumin

2 teaspoons sugar

2 teaspoons kosher salt

1 cup Almond Milk (recipe follows)
     or purchased coconut milk

To make the cilantro-mint sauce, combine all ingredients in a blender and puree at high speed until completely smooth. Reserve until needed. The sauce may be made a day or two in advance and kept covered in the refrigerator. This Thai-inspired herb puree makes more than enough for the sea bass; you need only about ¼ cup to use in this recipe. The remaining green puree goes well with steamed mussels, braised or grilled chicken, and is tasty spread on slabs of grilled sourdough.

almond milk

¼ pound sliced blanched almonds, lightly
     toasted and coarsely chopped

½ cinnamon stick

¼ lemon, thickly sliced

2 cups warm water

Soak the almonds, cinnamon stick, and lemon in the warm water for at least 2 hours or preferably, refrigerated, overnight. Using a blender, puree the almond mixture for 2 minutes, until smooth. Strain the almond milk through a fine-mesh sieve to remove any grittiness. Store in a tightly sealed container in the refrigerator until needed. The almond milk can be kept for several days.

INGREDIENT NOTE: ALMOND MILK

Almond milk, also known as Horchata in Latin America, is generally a refreshing drink made from soaked grains or nuts in water. Even though it has a creamy appearance, the "milk" is completely dairy free. Here the liquid is used in the cilantro puree, so we don't add any sugar. But as an alternative, the almond milk can easily be turned into a delicious beverage: add ½ cup of sugar, sprinkle with a small amount of ground cinnamon, and serve chilled.

The Lever House Cobb Salad is a very popular lunch item. We were looking to put a classic salad on the menu that people would respond to, and sure enough, this is a hit. At the restaurant we utilize ring molds to layer the salad components separately on top of each other. To build the tower of salad, we mound the BLT mixture on the bottom, stack the avocado/scallion combo on top, sprinkle with a layer of cheese, and finally garnish with watercress. For simplicity's sake, we've combined the salad elements all together for this recipe.

The Cobb Vinaigrette is a terrific multi-purpose vinaigrette; this recipe will make more dressing than you need and it's good to have on hand.

2 tablespoons fresh rosemary needles,
   chopped
3 garlic cloves, smashed
¼ cup extra-virgin olive oil
4 boneless chicken breasts (6 to 8 ounces
   each) with wings attached
8 slices bacon
Kosher salt and freshly ground black pepper
2 ripe Hass avocados, halved, pitted, peeled,
   and cut into 1-inch dice
Juice of 1 lime
1 bunch scallions, green and white parts,
   sliced (about 1½ cups)
½ cup Cobb Vinaigrette (recipe follows)
4 cups baby romaine lettuce, chiffonade
2 cups watercress, stems trimmed
16 cherry tomatoes, halved
¾ cup Stilton, or other good blue cheese,
   crumbled into large pieces

Combine the rosemary, garlic, and oil; rub on the chicken and marinate it for 1 hour.

Place a large grill pan or cast-iron skillet over medium heat. Grill the strips of bacon until crisp and drain on a paper towel–lined plate. Cut the bacon into 1-inch pieces.

Brush off the rosemary rub from the chicken, so it doesn't burn on the grill; season both sides of the chicken breasts with a generous amount of salt and pepper. Lay the chicken breasts skin side down in the hot pan and sear for 8 to 10 minutes, rotating them halfway through cooking to "mark" them. Turn the chicken over and grill the other side for 4 to 6 more minutes.

Lightly toss the diced avocado with the lime juice to prevent browning; make sure the pieces are coated evenly and the avocado doesn't smash like guacamole. Add the scallions, season with salt and pepper, and dress with 2 tablespoons of the cobb vinaigrette; toss gently to combine.

In a mixing bowl, combine the BLT salad: the bacon, lettuce, watercress, and tomatoes; and dress with about ¼ cup of the remaining vinaigrette. Add the avocado/scallion mixture and crumbled blue cheese; season with salt and pepper to taste. Toss to distribute the ingredients evenly.

To serve, divide the salad among 4 plates. Detach the chicken wings from the breasts. Slice the chicken breasts on the bias and fan around each salad. Lean the wings against the salad and drizzle the chicken with the remaining cobb vinaigrette.

cobb vinaigrette

MAKES ABOUT 1½ CUPS

1½ teaspoons Dijon mustard
1 garlic clove
¼ teaspoon sugar
2 tablespoons water
¼ cup red wine vinegar
1 teaspoon freshly squeezed lemon juice
1 teaspoon Worcestershire sauce
Generous pinch of kosher salt and freshly
   ground black pepper
¼ cup extra-virgin olive oil
¾ cup canola oil

Combine in a blender the mustard, garlic, sugar, water, vinegar, lemon juice, Worcestershire, salt, and pepper. Puree at high speed until well mixed. With the motor running, slowly drizzle in the oils to emulsify; taste and adjust seasoning if needed. Cover and keep in the refrigerator for up to 1 week.

GRILLED LAMB CHOPS WITH SWISS CHARD—HERB FRITTATA AND PIQUILLO VINAIGRETTE

For this recipe, the lamb chops are frenched all the way down to the eye of the meat—which involves completely trimming the layers of fat and a thin layer of skin that surround the eye and scraping the bones. You may want to have this done by your butcher—it's part of what butchers do; take advantage of their ability. The lamb is best if you marinate it for several hours, so plan accordingly.

Think of this frittata as greens with eggs, not eggs with greens. The eggs just hold it together so it sets up. Serve any leftover for brunch or pass out wedges of this vibrant-green egg dish as a rustic hors d'oeuvre with a smear of pesto or fines herbes (page 103) spread on top. The Spanish-inspired piquillo vinaigrette lends an exotic flair to other delightful standards, such as grilled shrimp, fish cakes, and chicken wings. Although the chops shouldn't be grilled until you are ready to eat, the vinaigrette and the frittata can be made hours in advance.

2 tablespoons sherry vinegar
3 tablespoons extra-virgin olive oil
2 fresh thyme sprigs
2 fresh oregano sprigs
3 garlic cloves, smashed
Pinch of red pepper flakes
12 rib lamb chops, excess fat trimmed,
  bones frenched, meat lightly pounded
½ cup Piquillo Vinaigrette (recipe follows)
Swiss Chard—Herb Frittata (recipe follows)
Chopped fresh chives, for garnish

In a glass or plastic container, mix the marinade: the vinegar, oil, thyme, oregano, garlic, and red pepper flakes. Put the lamb chops in the marinade, cover, and refrigerate for at least 2 hours or up to overnight, whatever you have time for. Take the lamb out of the refrigerator about 30 minutes before cooking to come to room temperature.

Place a large grill pan on 2 burners over medium-high heat or preheat an outdoor gas or charcoal grill until very hot. Remove the herbs from the meat, so they won't burn on the grill. Lay the lamb chops on the hot grill, and sear for 2 to 3 minutes on each side, rotating them halfway through cooking to "mark" them.

To serve, squeeze decorative stripes of the piquillo vinaigrette across the base of 4 plates. Place a wedge of the Swiss chard–herb frittata on the vinaigrette, lean 3 grilled chops against the frittata, with the bone facing up, and shower with chopped chives.

piquillo vinaigrette

MAKES ABOUT 1 CUP

¾ cup extra-virgin olive oil

3 garlic cloves, slivered

1 (13-ounce) can piquillo peppers, drained and
    coarsely chopped

Kosher salt and freshly ground black pepper

2 to 3 tablespoons sherry vinegar

Coat a small sauté pan with ¼ cup of oil and heat over medium-low flame. Sweat the garlic in the oil for 5 minutes, until tender but not brown or burnt. Add the piquillo peppers and cook, stirring, until it is heated through and the flavors meld, about 10 more minutes; season with salt and pepper. Transfer the peppers and garlic to a blender, puree until smooth. With the motor running, slowly pour in the remaining ½ cup of oil to emulsify the vinaigrette. Add the vinegar and blend just for another few seconds to incorporate; taste and season with salt and pepper if needed. Spoon the piquillo vinaigrette into a plastic squeeze bottle for serving and reserve at room temperature. Keep any leftover vinaigrette covered in the refrigerator for up to 3 days.

swiss chard–herb frittata

SERVES 4 (MAKES ONE 9-INCH FRITTATA)

1 pound Swiss chard, tough stems removed,
    leaves washed and cut in wide ribbons

1 onion, finely chopped

4 large eggs, lightly beaten

½ cup freshly grated Parmigiano-Reggiano

4 fresh basil leaves, chiffonade

1 tablespoon chopped fresh flat-leaf parsley
    leaves

1 teaspoon chopped fresh marjoram leaves

Generous pinch of kosher salt and freshly
    ground black pepper

2 tablespoons extra-virgin olive oil, plus more
    for serving

Fleur de sel

Preheat the oven to 275°F.

In a large bowl, combine the chard, onion, eggs, cheese, basil, parsley, and marjoram; season with a fair amount of salt and pepper. Brush a nonstick, ovenproof, 9–inch sauté pan with 1 tablespoon of the oil. Pour the chard mixture into the pan and smooth out the surface with a spatula. The pan will look very full and overflowing but the greens will cook down. Bake for 25 minutes, until the mixture is almost set.

Invert a plate over the skillet and carefully flip the frittata over onto the plate. Add the remaining tablespoon of oil to the pan and gently slide the frittata back in. Continue to bake for another 5 minutes, until completely set but not dried out. Cut the frittata into wedges and serve hot or at room temperature. Drizzle each piece with a little olive oil and sprinkle with fleur de sel.

GRILLED LAMB CHOPS WITH SWISS CHARD–HERB FRITTATA AND PIQUILLO VINAIGRETTE

This is my version of a summer clambake; the seasonal nature of the ingredients shows off the farm stand freshness of the sunny produce. At Lever House, we serve 1½ tails per customer; if you'd like to do so, use 6 lobsters instead of 4. The lobster spice mix will make more than you need to pull off this recipe, but it is hard to grind less. The unexpected exotic notes of the spices also go really well sprinkled on shrimp or butternut squash/pumpkin soup. To dry out the vanilla bean so it grinds up well into a powder, let it dry on the counter overnight or put it in the oven overnight, with just the pilot light on. If pressed for time, place the vanilla on a sheet pan and bake in a preheated 300°F oven for 5 to 10 minutes, until dried. Store in an airtight container until needed.

4 live lobsters (1½ pounds each)

1 tablespoon sea salt

¼ cup melted unsalted butter

Kosher salt and freshly ground black pepper

1 tablespoon Lobster Spice Mix
   (recipe follows)

1 tablespoon extra-virgin olive oil

2 tablespoons unsalted butter

5 scallions, green and a little of the white
   parts, finely sliced

4 ears sweet white corn, shucked, kernels
   cut from the cob (about 2 cups)

12 cherry tomatoes, halved

8 fresh basil leaves, chiffonade

To cook the lobsters, fill a large stockpot three-quarters of the way with water and add the sea salt; bring to a rapid boil over medium-high heat. Carefully ease 2 lobsters into the boiling water, and cook for 2 minutes; they will not be cooked through at this point. Using tongs, carefully remove the lobsters from the pot and plunge them in a large bowl of ice water for at least 5 minutes to ensure they are cool all the way through. Bring the pot of salt water back up to a boil and repeat with the remaining 2 lobsters.

Working with rubber gloves, use a sort of sideways twist to break the tails off of the bod-ies; it's best to do this over a sink since it can be messy. Bring the water back up to a boil and continue to cook the claws and knuckles for an additional 5 minutes (reserve the lobster bod-ies for stock or discard).

Using a big sharp knife, split the tails in half lengthwise, keeping them in the shell. If there are any visible veins or roe along the top of the tail, gently wash them away with cold water. Reserve the cleaned tails well wrapped in plas-tic in the coldest part of the refrigerator until needed. Cleaning and boiling the lobsters may be done a day in advance.

Place the claws and knuckles on the work surface, whack them open, remove the shells, and carefully pick out the meat with your fin-gers and chop it in large pieces. Reserve the claw and knuckle meat for the corn mixture.

Preheat the broiler.

Brush the split lobster tails with melted but-ter and season with kosher salt, pepper, and a pinch of the lobster spice mix. Put the lobster tails on a sheet pan and broil for about 4 min-utes, until slightly charred on the edges. Alter-natively, grill the lobsters face down on an outdoor grill or on a grill pan. Free the lobster tails from the shells by slipping a spoon under-neath the meat and giving a little pull, so it will be easier for guests to eat. Hold warm.

Place a nonstick pan over medium heat and add the oil and butter. When the butter begins to foam, add the scallions and sauté them for 2 to 3 minutes, just until they wilt. Add the corn and sauté for 2 to 3 minutes; season lightly with salt and pepper. Fold in the lobster claw and knuckle meat, toss gently to combine and heat the lobster through, about 2 to 3 more minutes. Mix in the cherry tomatoes and basil and check the seasoning.

To serve, spoon the corn mixture among 4 plates and then place 1 grilled lobster tail on top of each pile of vegetables.

lobster spice mix

MAKES ABOUT 3 TABLESPOONS

½ vanilla bean, dried

2 cinnamon sticks, halved

1 teaspoon freshly grated nutmeg

4 teaspoons whole allspice

6 whole cloves

1 teaspoon cayenne

1 teaspoon sugar

Combine the vanilla, cinnamon, nutmeg, all-spice, cloves, cayenne, and sugar in a spice mill or clean coffee grinder; buzz until the spices and sugar are a fine powder.

Berkshire pork and Kurobuta pork are the same thing—an heirloom breed regarded highly for its superior flavor and marbling of meat. If you've never tasted it before, it will be a revelation. The brine used here is the same as in the Braised Pork Belly. Plan to brine the chops overnight for maximum flavor. Sweet sauces paired with pork is a timeless combination. The spiciness of the curry and cloves give the fruit chutney a nice balance. Although the chutney recipe is large, it freezes well (it keeps up to three months) and makes a wonderful gift.

4 double-cut pork rib chops (12 ounces each), bone in, preferably free-range or Berkshire, tied

Brine (page 91)

½ tablespoon whole allspice

2 tablespoons coriander seed

½ teaspoon cumin seed

1 tablespoon juniper berries

1 teaspoon whole black peppercorns

Extra-virgin olive oil, for brushing the grill

Glazed Onions and New Potatoes (recipe follows)

½ cup Spiced Pineapple and Kumquat Chutney (recipe follows)

Watercress, for garnish

Submerge the pork chops in the brine, cover, and refrigerate for 8 hours or overnight to tenderize the meat. Remove the pork chops from the brine and pat dry with paper towels.

To make the aromatic spice mix, heat a small dry skillet over low flame and toast the allspice, coriander, cumin, juniper, and peppercorns for just a minute to release the fragrant oils; shake the pan so the mix doesn't scorch. In a spice mill or clean coffee grinder, buzz the toasted spices to a coarse powder. Season the pork chops liberally with the ground spice mix. There's no need to add salt because the salt in the brine penetrated the meat all the way through.

Place a large grill pan on 2 burners over medium-high heat or preheat an outdoor gas or charcoal grill until very hot. Brush oil on the grill to prevent sticking. Lay the pork chops on the hot grill, and sear for 7 to 8 minutes on each side, rotating them halfway through cooking to "mark" them. The chops will have a deep dark brown color (because of the sugar in the brine). Let the meat rest for 5 to 10 minutes in order to allow the juices to recirculate before cutting off the twine and serving.

To serve, divide the onions and potatoes among 4 plates, rest a pork chop on the vegetable "pillow," and dollop the chutney next to the chop. Garnish with a little watercress.

glazed onions and new potatoes

SERVES 4

¼ cup (½ stick) unsalted butter

12 cipollini onions, peeled (or substitute pearl onions)

12 red new potatoes, scrubbed and halved

Kosher salt and freshly ground black pepper

1 quart Chicken Stock (page 233), or as needed, warm

5 fresh sage leaves, chiffonade

In a large sauté pan over medium heat, melt the butter. Before the butter foams, lay the onions and potatoes in the pan in a single layer. Sauté for 5 minutes to warm the vegetables and coat them in the melted butter. Season with salt and pepper. Keep the potatoes and onions moving around the hot pan so they don't get too much color.

Add the stock to the vegetables in ½ cup increments. Continue stirring occasionally as the stock is absorbed, and adding a little bit more stock before the liquid is totally gone. Keep this up, and after about 10 minutes, begin to check the potatoes and onions for doneness (a sharp paring knife should pierce a potato with only a small amount of resistance).

Taste for seasoning, sprinkle with the chopped sage, and toss to combine before serving.

spiced pineapple and kumquat chutney

MAKES 1½ QUARTS

2 teaspoons whole cardamom pods

6 whole cloves

2 teaspoons Szechwan peppercorns

1 tablespoon ground ginger

2 teaspoons curry powder

Pinch of freshly grated nutmeg

2½ cups white wine vinegar

1 pineapple, peeled and cut in 1-inch dice

2 to 3 ripe pears, such as Bartlett, peeled and diced

1½ pounds kumquats, halved lengthwise, seeded, and quartered

2 cups sugar

Heat a small dry skillet over low flame and toast the cardamom, cloves, and peppercorns for just a minute to release the fragrant oils; shake the pan so they don't scorch. In a spice mill or clean coffee grinder, buzz the toasted spices to a coarse powder. Put the spice powder in a large saucepan and add the ginger, curry, nutmeg, and vinegar. Heat over medium flame for 5 to 8 minutes.

Fold in the fruit and simmer for 30 minutes, stirring frequently, to stew the fruit. Sprinkle in the sugar, and continue to simmer for 10 additional minutes, until the sugar is dissolved and the compote is thick and chunky. As a variation, for a different texture, puree the chutney to make a smooth sauce. The sauce may be served hot or cold.

CÔTE DE BOEUF

CÔTE DE BOEUF—STEAK FOR TWO SERVES 2

Thankfully, there's not a huge grocery list required to pull off this impressive dish, just a prime cut of beef and a very hot oven.

Besides picking up a good steak, this recipe is fairly easy, without a lot of components.

Order the thick rib eye steak ahead of time; this is where having a relationship with your local butcher comes in very handy.

Dry-aged beef is preferable for this dish. The process concentrates the natural flavors of the meat by allowing moisture to evaporate, making the meat more unctuous (and expensive). The term *prime beef* refers to the grade of fat marbling within the muscle.

For a very hearty meal, serve with Potato Gratin (page 175) or Brussels Sprouts with Pancetta (page 160) as sides.

2½ pounds (40 ounces) bone-in rib eye steak (preferably dry-aged prime beef), fat trimmed, bone frenched
Kosher salt and freshly ground black pepper
Fleur de sel

Disconnect the smoke detectors and open the windows.

Remove the steak from the refrigerator about 30 minutes before cooking so it is not too cold when you put it in the oven.

Preheat the oven to 450°F. Put a large cast-iron skillet in the oven to heat up as well.

Tie the rib eye around the side with butcher's twine to hold the shape of the steak or ask the butcher to do this for you. Season the steak liberally with salt and pepper on all sides; you should see the seasoning on the meat. Open the oven, put the steak in the preheated pan, close the door, and do not peek for 15 minutes.

Carefully take the meat out of the pan, and tip off the rendered fat that has accumulated. Return the steak to the pan, flipping it over, so the underside is now facing up. Roast for 15 minutes more.

Again, remove the steak from the pan and pour out the fat so it doesn't fry. Turn the steak on its side and sear the outer edge all the way around, rotating the steak every 5 minutes to caramelize the rim; this should take about another 15 minutes. The steak will be medium-rare and have an even brown color and crispy fat. Between all the roasting and rotating, the whole cooking process will take about 45 minutes.

Remove the steak to a cutting board, cover to keep warm, and let rest for at least 10 minutes to allow the juices to recirculate. Cut off the twine and, slicing parallel to the bone, cut the steak on a slight angle into ½-inch slices. Transfer the steak to a platter and set the bone alongside for presentation (the bone is perfect for Fido to gnaw on after dinner). Sprinkle the steak with fleur de sel, pour any accumulated meat juices from the cutting board over the top, and enjoy. (Don't forget to reactivate the smoke alarms.)

GRILLED SWORDFISH WITH CITRUS AND PISTACHIOS SERVES 4

Grilled swordfish is almost a primal memory for me. I can remember many summer dinners by the ocean eating swordfish seasoned with salt and freshly ground pepper, drizzled with olive oil and freshly squeezed lemon.

Although there aren't a lot of ingredients in the sauce, it has a complex flavor that works well with the grilled fish. At the restaurant we use Persian or Sicilian pistachios for their incomparable flavor and stunningly green color. Serve this simply impressive Mediterranean dish accompanied by sautéed spinach if desired.

½ cup golden raisins
2 tablespoons unsalted butter
2 garlic cloves, smashed
1 teaspoon red pepper flakes
1 tablespoon all-purpose flour
½ cup dry white wine, such as Pinot Grigio
½ cup Fish Stock (page 232)
1½ teaspoons fennel seeds
1 tablespoon finely grated zest and ½ cup juice from 1 navel orange
Juice of 1 lemon
4 swordfish steaks (6 ounces each)
Extra-virgin olive oil, for coating the fish
Kosher salt and freshly ground black pepper
1 teaspoon fennel seeds, ground
3 tablespoons pistachios, coarsely chopped, for garnish

Put the raisins in a small bowl and cover with warm water, soak for 10 minutes so they plump up, and then drain.

Place a deep sauté pan over medium heat and add the butter. When the butter is foamy, add the garlic and red pepper flakes; sauté for 1 minute to infuse the flavor into the butter.

When the garlic begins to color, remove it and discard.

Sprinkle in the flour, stirring constantly with a wooden spoon to prevent lumps and to cook out the raw taste, about 1 minute. Add the wine, fish stock, plumped raisins, whole fennel seeds, and the orange zest. Simmer for 5 minutes to heat everything up, then add the orange and lemon juices. Reduce the heat to low and continue to gently simmer for 20 minutes, until the sauce has thickened slightly, stirring occasionally.

Brush the swordfish with oil and season on both sides with salt, pepper, and ground fennel.

Place a large grill pan on 2 burners over medium-high heat or preheat an outdoor gas or charcoal grill until it is very hot. Grill the swordfish for 3 minutes on each side, to medium doneness.

To serve, place the grilled swordfish on each plate, drizzle the sauce over the fish, and garnish with chopped pistachios for a little crunch.

At Lever House, we use cuts of genuine Black Angus beef sirloin that weigh 12 to 14 ounces on average, but prime dry-aged steaks are also a wise choice. The wine merchant's butter is a compound butter similar to maitre d' butter or garlic butter. Compound butters allow you to customize different flavors, which gives grilled meats a whole new dimension. Try this one on grilled swordfish, tuna, or steamed vegetables.

These giant fries need a little more time and attention than regular French fries. The lower temperature gives the inside time to cook before the outside browns. Fortunately, you can blanch or parcook the fries most of the way through earlier in the day, so that cooking time is relatively short.

4 boneless Black Angus sirloin steaks or New York strips (10 to 12 ounces each), about 1½ inches thick
1 tablespoon extra-virgin olive oil, plus more for coating the steaks
Kosher salt and freshly ground black pepper
2 cups watercress, stems trimmed
Steak Fries (recipe follows)
¼ cup Wine Merchant's Butter (recipe follows)

Brush the steaks with oil and season both sides generously with salt and pepper; you should see the seasoning on the meat.

Place a large grill pan on 2 burners over medium-high heat or preheat an outdoor gas or charcoal grill until very hot.

Lay the steaks on the hot grill, and sear for 4 to 5 minutes on each side, rotating them halfway through cooking to "mark" them. Don't overcook; you want the steaks slightly charred on the outside and rare inside. Remove the steaks to a plate or cutting board, and let them rest for 10 minutes to allow the juices to recirculate. Serve the steaks whole or cut on the bias into ½-inch-thick slices.

To serve, put the watercress in a mixing bowl, drizzle with 1 tablespoon of olive oil, and season lightly with salt and pepper. Toss gently using your hands. Divide the cress among 4 plates, laying a steak on top of each pile. Stack 6 fries on each plate entwined like Lincoln Logs in a crosshatch formation. Top the steaks with wine merchant's butter and serve.

wine merchant's butter

MAKES ABOUT 1½ CUPS

½ bottle dry red wine (about 2 cups)
2 large shallots, minced
5 anchovy fillets, coarsely chopped
¼ cup coarsely chopped flat-leaf parsley
1 pound (4 sticks) unsalted butter, cut in chunks
¼ cup Veal Demi-Glace (page 231 or store-bought)
Fleur de sel and freshly ground black pepper
Pinch of Aleppo pepper or cayenne (see Ingredient Note, page 49)

In a saucepan over medium heat combine the wine and shallots and reduce by two-thirds, to about ½ cup. Cool down the mixture for 10 minutes.

In a food processor, combine the wine/shallot reduction with the anchovies, parsley, and butter; process until well mixed and tinted red. Add the veal demi-glace and pulse briefly a couple of times, until the ingredients are well blended.

Transfer the merchant's butter to a bowl; season with fleur de sel, black pepper, and Aleppo; mix with a spatula so the texture of the salt remains coarse.

Chill the butter in the fridge for 30 minutes. The wine merchant's butter can be made in advance and kept in the refrigerator or freezer for several weeks.

steak fries

MAKES 24 FRIES

Canola oil, for deep frying

6 large Idaho potatoes

Sea salt

Heat 3 inches of the oil in a deep fryer to 300°F. Alternatively, you can use a deep, heavy pot or pan along with a deep-frying or candy thermometer.

Peel the potatoes and cut off all sides to make a large, rectangular block. Cut the block in half lengthwise, and then cut them in half again lengthwise. You should wind up with 4 large Lincoln log–like pieces per potato, approximately 1 inch square by 4 inches long . . . they're huge.

Put the potatoes in a fryer basket or strainer and lower into the hot oil; do this in batches to avoid overcrowding and to keep the oil temperature constant. Fry for 10 minutes; the potatoes should not be crisp or fully cooked at this point, just a bit limp. Remove all the fries to a paper towel–lined platter to drain (this step may be done several hours before you need to finish cooking the fries).

Crank the oil temperature up to 360°F. Working in batches, fry the potatoes for 3 to 5 minutes, until they are golden brown and crispy, removing the cooked ones to a paper towel–lined platter to drain before adding the next batch. Season lightly with salt while the steak fries are still hot and serve.

LEVER HOUSE
LEVER BROTHERS COMPANY
1951
SKIDMORE OWINGS & MERRILL
ARCHITECTS
GEORGE A. FULLER COMPANY
BUILDERS

SIDES

Vegetables play an important role on the menu at Lever House. They are an integral part of how we do what we do and how we do it so well. I have worked hard to cultivate relationships with an ever-widening group of farmers and purveyors to supply us with the highest-quality fruits and vegetables available.

The Union Square Greenmarket, being a stone's throw from the restaurant, has also been a great source of inspiration. It is always exciting to see the first local strawberries, corn, or squash blossoms at farmers' stands—and challenging to try to think of great ways to showcase these products. Sometimes, the best thing we can do is quite simple, such as haricots verts with shallots and butter (page 169). And then sometimes it can be fun (and quite tasty!) to do something a bit more elaborate, like our potato gratin (page 175). Whichever sides you ultimately decide to make, be sure that the ingredients are fresh, and that you give their cooking and seasoning the attention that is their due.

BRUSSELS SPROUTS WITH PANCETTA SERVES 4

Nutty Brussels sprouts and salty pork fat are two great tastes that taste great together. The

sweet shallots add a hearty dimension to the classic duo. These Brussels sprouts can be

cooked from raw (and will caramelize a bit more) but blanching them will cut

down considerably on the cooking time. If you can't find pancetta,

slab bacon makes a more-than-acceptable substitute. This

easy side dish is a holiday favorite that's sure to please.

CAULIFLOWER PUREE SERVES 4

1 tablespoon extra-virgin olive oil
3 ounces pancetta, cut in very small dice
3 shallots, minced
1½ pounds Brussels sprouts (about
    24 Brussels sprouts), root ends
    trimmed, halved lengthwise
Kosher salt and freshly ground black pepper
1 tablespoon chopped fresh flat-leaf parsley

Place a large sauté pan over medium heat and coat with the oil. When the oil is hot, add the pancetta and cook for 3 to 5 minutes, stirring occasionally, until crispy. Add the shallots and continue to cook for 2 more minutes, until they begin to soften. Remove the pancetta-shallot mixture to a side plate with a slotted spoon, leaving in the pan as much of the oil and rendered pancetta fat as possible.

Raise the heat to high and add the Brussels sprouts to the pan, season with salt and pepper, and sauté, stirring from time to time, for 7 to 8 minutes. The sprouts should begin to brown and soften a bit.

At this point, add the reserved pancetta-shallot mixture to the pan, stirring to mix well, and cook for an additional minute or two. Finally, add the chopped parsley, toss everything together, taste and adjust the seasoning, and serve.

I love cauliflower. It is decidedly unlike broccoli, although they are always linked. Roasted florets braised with tomato sauce or this really delicious and simple puree prove that cauliflower is quite versatile. At the restaurant we often serve butter-poached Nantucket Bay scallops on a bed of cauliflower puree and garnish with a few pieces of uni (sea urchin roe).

1¼ pounds cauliflower florets
    (about 1 head of cauliflower)
¼ cup milk
¼ cup heavy cream
Kosher salt and freshly ground black pepper

Put the cauliflower in a medium saucepan and pour in the milk; place over low heat and cover. Simmer for 15 minutes, until the cauliflower steams in the milk and the florets become tender. Transfer the mixture to a blender.

In a small pot, bring the heavy cream to a boil. Pour the hot cream into the blender with the cauliflower and milk. Puree until smooth and be sure to hold down the lid with a towel for safety. Season with salt and pepper and serve immediately.

CARROTS GLAZED WITH GINGER AND ORANGE SERVES 4

If you can find heirloom baby carrots—red, white, yellow, nuggets, etc.—please use them. We get our carrots from a small farm on Long Island named Satur Farms. These glazed carrots are a melodic balance of vegetable sweetness, citrusy tang, and just the right amount of heat (from the ginger and Aleppo pepper). The carrots can be glazed hours before you need them and then gently reheated. Don't add the mint until just before serving.

3 tablespoons unsalted butter

1½ pounds baby carrots, peeled, ½ inch of green top left on, halved lengthwise

Kosher salt and freshly ground black pepper

½ teaspoon Aleppo pepper (see Ingredient Note, page 49) or cayenne

1½ teaspoons freshly grated ginger

1 cup freshly squeezed orange juice

2 teaspoons fresh lime juice

4 large fresh mint leaves, chiffonade

In a sauté pan large enough to hold the carrots in one layer, melt the butter over medium heat. Add the carrots and season lightly with salt, pepper, and Aleppo, tossing well to combine. Reduce the heat slightly and sauté the carrots for 3 to 4 minutes. If the carrots are very fresh, the salt will draw out a little of their moisture.

Stir in the grated ginger and add a third of the orange juice. Continue to cook the carrots, stirring from time to time. As the o.j. evaporates and cooks down, add a bit more in increments. Repeat until the carrots are tender and the juice has reduced to a syrupy glaze, about 10 to 12 minutes (see Note). Taste the carrots; they should be just cooked through and not mushy.

Just before serving, drizzle the lime juice over the carrots to balance out the sweetness of the o.j. Sprinkle the mint ribbons on top to garnish and serve.

NOTE

If the carrots are cooked before the o.j. has reduced to a glaze, remove them from the pan with a slotted spoon, quickly reduce the liquid to a glaze, and then add the carrots back to the pan. If the carrots are not fully cooked by the time all the o.j. has reduced into a glaze, add small amounts of water to the pan and continue cooking until they are.

FAVA, PECORINO, AND MINT SALAD SERVES 4

A true sign of spring, fresh fava beans are greenish legumes that look like large lima beans. In fact, limas work just as well in this recipe if you prefer them or can't find fava beans. Sometimes known as broad beans, favas are very popular in Mediterranean and Middle Eastern dishes. We put this salad on the menu from May to August. It makes a tasty light lunch or side dish. Serve this with Colorado Rack of Lamb with Stuffed Piquillo Peppers (page 112). Ten anchovies may seem like a lot for a dressing—cut back on them if you must—but they really work as a wonderful mélange with the cheese and mint.

2 pounds fresh fava beans
2 cups baby arugula, rinsed and dried
4 fresh mint leaves, chiffonade
Kosher salt and freshly ground black pepper
3 to 4 tablespoons Anchovy Vinaigrette (recipe follows)
1 (2-ounce) wedge of pecorino, finely grated

To blanch the fava beans for the salad, bring a large pot of lightly salted water to a boil. Shell the favas from the pods and boil the beans for 2 minutes. Drain the beans and plunge in an ice bath to "shock" them, i.e., to stop the cooking process and cool them down right away. Slip off the tough outer skins of the beans and discard them; put the beans in a large bowl.

To assemble the salad, combine in a bowl the blanched fava beans, arugula, and mint. Season lightly with salt and pepper. Dress the salad with 3 to 4 tablespoons of the vinaigrette and gently toss using your hands to combine. Add a little more than half of the grated cheese and lightly toss again.

Divide the salad among 4 plates, trying to equally distribute the arugula and the goodies for each portion. Sprinkle the rest of the cheese on top of the salads and finish off with a final grind of black pepper.

anchovy vinaigrette
MAKES 1¼ CUPS
10 anchovy fillets
5 garlic cloves
½ cup sherry vinegar
Freshly ground black pepper
½ cup extra-virgin olive oil

To make the vinaigrette, put the anchovies and garlic in a blender and puree well. While the motor is still running, add the vinegar and season with pepper. Now, slowly drizzle in the olive oil until the dressing thickens. Reserve at room temperature until ready to use. This vinaigrette keeps covered for a couple of days in the refrigerator, so if you want to make it ahead of time, just whisk it back together before dressing the salad.

This recipe makes more chili oil than you will need for this amount of broccoli raab, but garlic-chili oil is important to have at your disposal. It's delicious on fish, steaks, or grilled vegetables, and ideal drizzled on pasta with a little freshly chopped parsley and grated Parmigiano-Reggiano. Serve this side with Pan-Seared Veal Chops with Chanterelles and Madeira (page 122).

Kosher salt

1½ pounds broccoli raab, stems trimmed, washed well

½ cup extra-virgin olive oil

3 garlic cloves, smashed

½ teaspoon red pepper flakes

Freshly ground black pepper

To blanch the broccoli raab, bring a large pot of well-salted water to a rolling boil (it should taste like sea water). Boil the broccoli raab for 2 to 3 minutes. Drain and plunge it in an ice bath to "shock" it, i.e., to stop the cooking process and cool it down right away. This procedure also sets the vibrant green color of the broccoli. The raab should be a little limp but not cooked all the way through. Drain the blanched raab well. Blanching the broccoli raab may be done hours in advance if you wish.

Heat a large sauté pan over low flame and film with the oil. When the oil gets hazy, add the garlic cloves. Shimmy the pan over the burner, until the garlic becomes light golden. Sprinkle in the red pepper flakes and sauté for 20 to 30 seconds, being careful not to burn the chili flakes or they can become bitter. Allow the chili oil to cool with the solids and then strain it once it has cooled down.

When you are ready to serve the broccoli raab, preheat a charcoal grill or a large cast-iron skillet. Put the broccoli raab in a large bowl, season generously with salt and pepper and drizzle over a scant ¼ cup of the chili oil. Toss well to combine and coat the raab with the oil. Lift the raab from the bowl and put it on the hot grill or pan and move it around with a pair of tongs so that it heats through and begins to brown a little bit. This procedure should take only a few minutes, perhaps 3 or 4.

Place the grilled broccoli raab on a serving platter, season with a bit more salt and pepper, drizzle with a little more chili oil, and enjoy.

Haricots verts are a Lever House staple. Tossed with butter and shallots, the green beans are a simple pleasure. The pork butter, an amalgam of pork, garlic, and herbs, can be made in larger quantities and frozen. I like to call it butter because the cured pork fat takes on a butterlike consistency when it's pureed. It is a flavorful addition to lamb stew, sautéed potatoes, or fried eggs; the possibilities are endless. A unique Italian specialty, lardo is a cured meat made from the layer of fat found directly under the pig's skin, basically, salt-cured fatback that is similar to pancetta. Forgo the pork butter if you wish and serve the sweet green beans simply with the shallots.

1 pound haricots verts or thin green beans, stems trimmed
3 tablespoons unsalted butter
Kosher salt and freshly ground black pepper
2 large shallots, finely diced
2 tablespoons Pork Butter (recipe follows)

To blanch the haricots verts, bring a large pot of well-salted water to a boil (it should taste like sea water). Boil the beans for only 2 minutes (do this in batches to keep the water at a rolling boil if necessary). Drain the beans and plunge them in an ice bath to "shock" them, i.e., stop the cooking process and cool them down right away. This procedure also sets the vibrant color of the green beans. Drain the blanched beans and reserve in the refrigerator.

Place a deep sauté pan over medium-low heat. Heat 2 tablespoons of water and then swirl in the butter. This duo is classically called a beurre monte, and will coat the vegetables. Just make sure the butter and water don't boil, as the two may separate—oil and water don't naturally mix, after all.

Once the butter and water have become one and emulsified, add the blanched green beans. Coat the vegetables in the butter sauce for a minute or 2 to combine and just warm through; season lightly with salt and pepper. Add the diced shallots, toss and stir for another minute, until they soften; check the seasoning and adjust as needed.

Serve the haricots verts as is, or stir in 2 tablespoons of the pork butter just after you add the shallots. Cook until the pork fat begins to melt and sizzle, a few minutes more. Serve immediately.

pork butter

MAKES ABOUT 4 OUNCES
4½ ounces lardo or pancetta, diced and well chilled in the freezer for 20 minutes
1 large garlic clove, coarsely chopped
3 sprigs fresh marjoram or oregano, leaves only

Combine the lardo (or pancetta), garlic, and marjoram in a food processor. Use the pulse button and process until all the ingredients are chopped finely. However, be careful not to overwork the ingredients or the heat from the rapidly spinning processor blade will begin to melt the fat in the lardo, causing it to liquefy. Use immediately or cover and refrigerate for up to 2 weeks.

LEFT TO RIGHT: HARICOTS VERTS, SUGAR SNAP PEAS, AND OKRA

This side began its life as part of a composed salad. We served the fried okra atop a medley of green market beans dressed with a savory vinaigrette. People who think okra is slimy will be in for a pleasant surprise when they taste this dish. Folks in the South have popularized battering okra with cornmeal; tempura is our lighter adaptation.

Fried quickly in this way, the okra remains crisp and doesn't break down and become mushy. The lemon-Aleppo mayonnaise is a tart and punchy accompaniment to serve on the side for dipping, making this dish a wonderful finger food to accompany cocktails.

Canola oil, for deep frying
1¾ cups all-purpose flour,
**   plus 1 cup for dredging**
¾ cup cornstarch
2 tablespoons baking soda
1 tablespoon sugar
1½ teaspoons kosher salt
2 cups plus 2 tablespoons cold seltzer
Sea salt and freshly ground black pepper
¾ pound fresh okra, halved lengthwise
½ cup Lemon-Aleppo Mayonnaise
**   (recipe follows)**

In a large heavy pot or deep fryer, heat about 3 inches of canola oil to 375°F.

While the oil is heating up, make the tempura batter.

In a large bowl, mix 1¾ cups of the flour, the cornstarch, baking soda, sugar, and kosher salt. Whisk in the seltzer until a pancake batter consistency is achieved and there are no lumps. Put the remaining 1 cup of flour on a plate and season well with salt and pepper.

Dust the okra halves in the seasoned flour to coat. Shake off the excess. Dip the okra into the batter one by one to lightly coat completely, letting the excess drip back into the bowl. Gently lower each okra into the hot oil and fry them in batches; do not overcrowd the pan. The okra should sort of "fizz" when they hit the hot oil and will puff up fairly quickly. Fry the okra for 1 to 2 minutes and then use a slotted spoon or chopsticks to turn over the pieces so they cook evenly. When the coating is light golden brown and crisp, carefully remove the fried okra to a plate lined with paper towels to drain. While the tempura is still hot, lightly season with sea salt and serve immediately with the lemon-Aleppo mayonnaise.

lemon-aleppo mayonnaise

MAKES ABOUT ½ CUP
½ cup mayonnaise
1 teaspoon freshly squeezed lemon juice
1 teaspoon lemon zest, finely chopped
1 teaspoon Aleppo (see Ingredient Note, page 49) or cayenne pepper
Pinch of sea salt

To make the mayonnaise, combine all the ingredients in a bowl and mix well with a whisk or rubber spatula. Refrigerate until needed. This mayonnaise can be made several hours in advance and will keep overnight, but is best the same day it is made.

SUGAR SNAP PEAS WITH BROWN BUTTER AND SAGE **SERVES 4**

When sugar snap peas are in season, this recipe is a great way to take advantage of their sweetness by mingling them with nutty butter and herbaceous sage. If you want to cut down on the cooking time, you could blanch the beans first.

¼ cup (½ stick) unsalted butter
1 pound sugar snap peas, ends trimmed and
  strings removed
Kosher salt and freshly ground black pepper
4 fresh sage leaves, chiffonade

Place a large sauté pan over medium-high heat. When the pan is hot, add 3 tablespoons of butter and swirl it around. The butter will melt, then foam, and once the foam subsides, the butter will begin to brown and smell nutty. At this point, add the snap peas in a single layer; season with salt and pepper. Reduce the heat to medium-low and sauté the snap peas for 4 to 5 minutes, stirring occasionally, to coat in the brown butter. The pods will begin to brown a little bit and lose their raw taste. Add the remaining tablespoon of butter and sauté another minute or two. Finally, sprinkle in the sage and stir well to mix. Cook for another minute. The sage should sizzle a bit and emit a wonderful aroma. Serve the sugar snap peas immediately.

POTATO BLINI MAKES 25 TO 30 (2-INCH) BLINIS

At Lever House we make scads of silver dollar–size blinis at a time. An elegant way to serve hors d'ouevres, blini make a wonderful vehicle for an array of garnishes. The little potato pancakes are perfect finger food topped with dollops of crème fraîche and caviar, thin slices of smoked salmon, or trout. Try them with the Tasmanian Sea Trout Gravlax with Cucumber-Chive Relish (page 44). If you want to get a little creative, fold freshly chopped chives or freshly cut corn into the batter before cooking the blinis.

The batter can be made up to an hour before you need it, or the blinis may be cooked, wrapped in plastic, and frozen. Remove from the freezer an hour before needed and warm briefly in a 350°F oven.

Kosher salt
1 large Idaho potato
½ cup milk
1 cup all-purpose flour
2 teaspoons baking powder
Freshly ground black pepper
2 large eggs
1 large egg yolk
Approximately ½ cup melted unsalted butter

Peel the potato and cut it into even-size chunks. Put the potato pieces in a pot with well-salted cold water to cover, bring to a boil over medium-high heat, and simmer until the potatoes are thoroughly cooked and tender, about 15 minutes. Drain in a colander and allow to steam for a minute or two in order to let the moisture evaporate.

Pass the tender pieces of potato through a ricer or food mill. Measure out 1 cup of the mashed potatoes and put in a large bowl. Whisk the milk into the hot mashed potatoes to incorporate until soupy. Mix in the flour and baking powder, while continuing to whisk to combine into a shaggy dough; season with a generous dose of salt and pepper. Add the eggs, whisking some more, until the mixture forms a batter. Add the yolk and 3 tablespoons of melted butter; stir until the batter is smooth; it should resemble thick pancake batter.

The easiest and quickest way to form the blinis is to pour the batter into a homemade pastry bag, i.e. a resealable plastic bag with a corner cut off, and pipe it out into the pan; of course you may use an official pastry bag with a small tip if you have one.

To cook the blinis, heat a griddle or large nonstick pan over medium heat. Film the pan with about 1½ tablespoons of melted butter, swirling it around to coat the whole surface. Pipe out approximately 1 tablespoon of batter per blini into the hot pan, to make pancakes about 2 inches in diameter (about the size of a half dollar). Take care not to crowd the circles too close together. Cook until the bottoms are browned, about 1 minute. Gently flip over the blinis with a spatula and cook for another minute, until the pancakes have puffed up slightly. Add about a tablespoon of melted butter as you sauté the blinis in batches; continue until all of the batter is used up.

Put the blinis on a large platter and cover with a cloth napkin to keep warm. Top the pancakes with just about anything and serve them as soon as possible.

The Lever House potato gratin is very flavorful. If you don't like garlic, feel free to omit it. The gratin is not spicy, but if you don't like the flavor of cayenne, you can by all means lower the amount or omit it as well.

Before you get crazy cutting ingredients, though, try it this way once. I'm sure you will be hooked. Slice the potatoes right before using so they don't turn brown.

2 tablespoons unsalted butter
5 garlic cloves, thinly sliced
1 quart heavy cream, plus more as needed
3 fresh sage leaves, tied together with
   kitchen twine
Kosher salt and freshly ground black pepper
½ teaspoon cayenne pepper
Pinch of freshly grated nutmeg
5 large Idaho potatoes (about 3 pounds),
   peeled and reserved in cold water

Preheat the oven to 300°F.

Put the butter and garlic in a large saucepan and place over medium heat. Sweat the garlic for 2 to 3 minutes, until soft but not brown. Pour in the heavy cream, add the sage, and bring to a simmer; season with a generous amount of salt and pepper. Mix in the cayenne and nutmeg to infuse the cream with flavor.

Slice the potatoes thinly, into approximately ⅛-inch-thick pieces, using a chef's knife or mandoline. Add the potatoes to the simmering cream as quickly as possible to prevent them from discoloring. Simmer for 15 minutes, stirring gently with a rubber spatula, rotating the potatoes from the bottom to the top, for even cooking. Pierce the potatoes with a fork to check for doneness; they should still be really firm but not raw. Remove the sage bundle and discard. Taste the cream for seasoning and adjust as necessary—it should definitely taste well seasoned.

Using a slotted spoon, arrange the potatoes evenly in a large ovenproof casserole dish, pushing them down firmly to compress the air pockets. Pour the cream over the potatoes; if there is not enough liquid to go three-quarters of the way up the potatoes, then pour some additional cream on top to make up the difference.

Bake the potato gratin, uncovered, for 1 hour, until the potatoes are cooked through and the top begins to brown. Test for doneness by piercing the potatoes with a paring knife. If there is no resistance, they're done; otherwise, cook them for an additional 10 minutes.

Let the gratin set for 15 minutes before cutting into squares and serving. The resting time allows the potatoes to reabsorb the cream and helps the gratin hold its shape.

POTATO GRATIN

ROASTED ASPARAGUS SERVES 4

Roasted asparagus is an integral part of the Roasted Asparagus Salad with Shaved Manchego and Marcona Almonds appetizer (page 80), but the vegetable itself also makes a great side dish drizzled with balsamic vinegar. The asparagus are wonderful hot but may be cooked ahead and served at room temperature or chilled. For a special treat, garnish the roasted asparagus with slices of Serrano ham or serve them Italian style, alla Bismarck, with finely shaved curls of Parmigiano-Reggiano and a fried egg on top . . . a fantastic combination!

20 large asparagus spears (about 1½ bunches)
2 tablespoons extra-virgin olive oil
Sea salt and freshly ground black pepper
1 tablespoon balsamic vinegar

Preheat the oven to 400°F.

Cut or snap off about 1 inch of the tough bottom stem of the asparagus and discard. Using a vegetable peeler, shave off the outer skin of the lower half of the remaining stalk, keeping the tops intact.

Put the asparagus spears in a medium mixing bowl, coat with the oil, and season generously with salt and pepper. Spread out the asparagus in a single layer on a sheet pan. Roast them for 10 minutes, until tender but not colored. Drizzle the balsamic vinegar over the roasted asparagus, and adjust the seasoning if needed.

These roasted mushrooms are an easy and delicious side to serve with a nice piece of steak or veal roast. It is also an integral ingredient for the seared skate recipe on page 130.

$1\frac{1}{2}$ **pounds oyster and shiitake mushrooms, wiped of grit**
$\frac{1}{2}$ **Spanish onion, finely diced**
1 garlic clove
1 fresh thyme sprig
2 tablespoons extra-virgin olive oil
$\frac{1}{2}$ **cup Vegetable Stock (page 228)**
Kosher salt and freshly ground black pepper

Preheat the oven to 325°F.

Put the mushrooms in a large mixing bowl and combine with the onion, garlic, thyme, and oil. Toss to evenly distribute the ingredients. Spread the mushroom mixture in a roasting pan and pour in the stock; season well with salt and pepper. Cover the pan with aluminum foil and roast for 30 to 40 minutes, until the mushrooms are tender.

FINGERLING POTATOES SERVES 4

This simple potato recipe is a versatile all-

purpose side dish.

2 teaspoons sea salt

1 cup dry white wine, such as Sauvignon
   Blanc

2 bay leaves

1/2 pound fingerling potatoes, washed and
   sliced into 1/4-inch-thick coins

Bring a large pot of water to a boil; add the salt, wine, and bay leaves. Carefully put in the potatoes and simmer for 5 to 8 minutes, until they're cooked through but still retain their shape. Drain and serve.

SPICY EGGPLANT SERVES 4

Japanese and Chinese eggplants have fewer
seeds than the plumper Italian ones and are
commonly available in a number of markets.
This recipe is beyond simple and fits right in
as part of a mezze platter, along with the
Chickpea Puree (page 69) and some pita
wedges, or served as a bread spread on the
Roast Leg of Lamb Sandwich (page 124).

3 tablespoons saba/vin cotto (see Ingredient
   Note, page 60) or balsamic vinegar
3/4 teaspoon kosher salt
1/3 cup canola oil
1 pound Japanese eggplant, unpeeled,
   3/4-inch dice
1/2 teaspoon red pepper flakes
2 scallions, white and green parts, sliced on
   the bias

In a small bowl combine the saba and salt, mixing to dissolve the salt.

Place a large sauté pan over medium-high
heat and pour in the oil. When the oil gets hazy
and starts to shimmer, add the eggplant; fry
and toss for about 10 minutes, until the eggplant starts to soften and brown. Sprinkle the
eggplant with the red pepper flakes, tossing to
combine. Pour in the salted saba mixture, letting it bubble, and reduce slightly, until the
eggplant looks sticky. Fold in the scallions and
give the eggplant a final toss to combine. You
may serve it hot or cold.

GREEN HERB SPAETZLE SERVES 4

Literally translated from German as "little sparrow," spaetzle are tiny noodles, similar to a pasta. The spaetzle dough is forced through a sieve, colander, or spaetzle-maker with large holes (also called a spaetzle hex, a tool that looks like a grater without sharp edges). The tiny dumplings are poached before being pan-fried with butter or added to soups or other dishes (usually a good leftover idea). In Germany, spaetzle is served as a side dish much like potatoes or rice. It goes well with lots of entrée recipes in this book, such as the Alaskan Black Cod with Baby Bok Choy, Charred Fennel, and Red Onions (page 134) or the Grilled Lobster Tails with Sweet Corn, Cherry Tomatoes, and Basil (page 148), as we serve it at Lever House. The dough can be made up to a day in advance, as can cooked spaetzle. Of French origin, *fromage blanc* simply means "white cheese." It's a wonderfully creamy cheese that has the consistency of sour cream, along with the bright tartness.

4 large eggs
3 large egg yolks
¼ cup chopped fresh chives, plus
    2 tablespoons
¼ cup chopped fresh flat-leaf parsley, plus
    2 tablespoons
¼ cup chopped fresh chervil
1 cup fromage blanc, crème fraîche, farmer's
    cheese, or quark
2 cups all-purpose flour
Pinch of freshly grated nutmeg
2 teaspoons kosher salt
1 teaspoon freshly ground black pepper

Combine in a blender or food processor the eggs, yolks, and ¼ cup each of the chives, parsley, and chervil; puree until well mixed, 2 to 3 minutes. Pour the egg mixture into a large bowl. Add the fromage blanc and, using a sturdy whisk, mix until well combined.

Add the flour in increments to make the dough slightly sticky yet still elastic. Season with nutmeg, salt, and pepper. When well blended, add the remaining chopped chives and parsley. Do not overwork. Alternatively, the dough can be made in a standing electric mixer using a paddle attachment. Let the batter rest at least 1 hour before forming the spaetzle, so the gluten can relax.

Bring a large pot of well-salted water to a boil. To form the spaetzle, hold a large-holed colander (or a spaetzle-maker if you have one) over the simmering water and push the dough through the holes with a spatula or spoon. Do this in batches so you don't overcrowd the pot.

Cook for 2 minutes or until the spaetzle floats to the surface, stirring gently to prevent sticking. Use a strainer or spider to lift the noodles out of the water and quickly rinse with cool water. Make sure the pot of water returns to a boil before starting to cook another batch of spaetzle.

To serve, the spaetzle can be prepared in two ways, either sautéed in a large nonstick pan in brown butter or olive oil until crispy, or heated gently in beurre monte (an emulsion of 2 tablespoons water and 3 tablespoons butter; see instructions on page 169). Either method takes only a few minutes.

WALNUT AND GARLIC TAPENADE MAKES ABOUT 1½ CUPS

This chunky nut spread replaces butter on the table at Lever House. We serve the walnut-garlic tapenade to guests accompanied by flat focaccia called pizza bianca, hand-crafted by Jim Lahey at Sullivan St Bakery. Spread the tapenade on crostini, crackers, or fresh bread; the little bit of vinegar heightens the flavor and sets the whole thing off—it's addictive.

5 cloves Roasted Garlic Confit (page 234)
1 cup walnut pieces
1 tablespoon white wine vinegar
⅔ cup grapeseed oil
Kosher salt and freshly ground black pepper
2 teaspoons fresh chervil or flat-leaf parsley leaves
1 teaspoon fresh marjoram or oregano leaves

Combine the roasted garlic, walnuts, and vinegar in a food processor and pulse several times to make a coarse paste. Alternatively, the tapenade can be made by hand in a large mortar and pestle . . . with some elbow grease.

Slowly drizzle in the oil and pulse a few more times to emulsify. Season with salt and pepper. Fold in the chervil and marjoram by hand. The walnut and garlic tapenade may be served immediately or covered and refrigerated for up to 1 week. Bring the tapenade to room temperature before serving with bread.

SWEET POTATO AND GOLDEN RAISIN GRATIN SERVES 4 TO 8

This gratin had its start on the Lever House Thanksgiving Day menu. It went really well with our roast turkey and I'm sure it will with yours also. This would be quite tasty with pork chops, too.

1 cup apple cider

3 tablespoons apple cider vinegar

2 tablespoons dark rum (optional)

1 cinnamon stick

1 bay leaf

1 cup golden raisins

2 tablespoons unsalted butter

3 large sweet potatoes (about 3 pounds),
    peeled and sliced ⅛ inch thick

Kosher salt and freshly ground black pepper

3 cups heavy cream

In a small pot combine the cider, vinegar, rum (if you are using), cinnamon, and bay leaf; bring to a boil over medium heat.

Put the raisins in a glass bowl and pour the boiling liquid over them. Steep for 15 minutes to plump up the raisins and infuse with flavor. Drain the liquid and discard the cinnamon and bay leaf.

Preheat the oven to 300°F.

Butter the bottom and sides of a large ovenproof casserole dish. Sprinkle a third of the soaked raisins evenly in the dish, shingle a third of the sweet potatoes in an even layer over the raisins; season with salt and pepper. Repeat the layers 2 more times, until the ingredients are used up. The sweet potatoes are the last layer. Pour the heavy cream over the top; it should just barely cover the sweet potatoes.

Bake the sweet potato gratin, uncovered, for 1 hour, checking every 15 minutes or so and pressing down on the sweets with a spatula to keep them covered with cream so the top doesn't dry out. The gratin is done when the potatoes are tender and the cream has browned nicely on top. Let the sweet potato gratin rest for 15 minutes before cutting into squares and serving. The resting time allows the potatoes to reabsorb the cream and helps the gratin hold its shape.

DESSERTS

Our exceptionally talented pastry chef, Deborah Snyder, has made a selection of some of her most memorable desserts for this chapter.

With her innate ability to combine flavors, Deborah has come up with dishes that have an inner logic and taste great. Her ever-changing cookie plate—a great assortment of textures, temperatures, and flavors—has been widely imitated but never surpassed in quality. Many a busy night I've wandered over to her station to bum a few cookies to keep my blood sugar level up!

Some of the desserts are pictured here in individual portions, as we would serve them in the restaurant. For ease for your kitchen, however, the recipes have been adjusted to make one dessert that can be sliced into individual portions.

Deborah is particularly exacting about ingredients. Measure and weigh your ingredients carefully. Pastry is more of a science than savory cooking. Follow the recipes closely and you will achieve wonderful results and enjoy some delightful desserts.

APPLE CHEESECAKE CRISP SERVES 8

This special addition to the menu for New

Year's Eve 2003 and was so well received

that we served it for the duration of the win-

ter. The butterscotch cake is one we come

back to every fall, as its dark caramel tones

and soft moist crumb combine well with

almost any fall fruit, such as pear or quince.

The Apple Cheesecake Crisp is perfect for

company; it has four impressive layers: the

cake, cheesecake cream, caramel apples, and

crumble topping. If pressed for time, simply

serve the cake with the caramel apples on

the side. The crumb topping is an all-

purpose streusel. It may be made ahead and

stored, covered and unbaked, for several

days in the refrigerator, and can be used to

top coffee cakes, muffins, or even a pie.

CHEESECAKE CREAM

$1/2$ cup granulated sugar

$3^{1}/_{2}$ tablespoons cornstarch

8 large egg yolks ($3/4$ cup)

2 cups milk

Zest of 1 lemon, finely grated

$1/2$ vanilla bean

2 gelatin sheets or $1/2$ ($1/4$ ounce) envelope
   powdered unflavored gelatin

12 ounces cream cheese ($1^{1}/_{2}$ 8-ounce
   packages), at room temperature

$1/4$ teaspoon natural vanilla extract

BUTTERSCOTCH CAKE

2 cups (4 sticks) unsalted butter, cut in
   chunks

$3/4$ cup all-purpose flour

$3/4$ teaspoon baking powder

$1/2$ teaspoon baking soda

$1/2$ teaspoon salt

$1^{3}/_{4}$ cups dark brown sugar, lightly packed

2 large eggs

2 large egg yolks

1 tablespoon natural vanilla extract

$1/2$ cup buttermilk

CARAMEL APPLES

1 cup granulated sugar

2 tablespoons unsalted butter,
   cut in small pieces

$1/4$ cup heavy cream

5 tart, firm apples, such as Granny Smith,
   peeled, cored, and cut into $1/4$-inch slices

1 teaspoon ground cinnamon

$1/2$ teaspoon salt

CRISP TOPPING

$1^{1}/_{4}$ cups all-purpose flour

$1/2$ cup granulated sugar

$1/4$ teaspoon salt

$3/4$ teaspoon ground cinnamon

$1/2$ cup melted unsalted butter

1 teaspoon natural vanilla extract

Ice cream or whipped cream, for serving

To make the cheesecake cream, in a large mixing bowl, sift together the sugar and cornstarch. Add the yolks and whisk to dissolve the sugar and cornstarch.

In a small pot over medium-low heat, combine the milk and lemon zest. Scrape out the seeds of the vanilla bean and add them to the milk; add the pod for extra flavor. Bring the milk to a brief simmer to infuse with the aromatics; do not boil.

Temper the yolks by gradually whisking half of the hot vanilla milk into the yolk mixture. Do not add the hot milk too quickly or the eggs will cook and begin to scramble. Add the tempered eggs back into the pot of remaining milk and stir over medium heat, just until the mixture starts to boil. Remove from the heat.

Soften the gelatin sheets in cool water for 2 minutes, then remove and squeeze out excess water (if using powdered gelatin, soak in 2 tablespoons cool water for 3 minutes).

Add the bloomed gelatin to the hot milk-and-egg mixture off the stove, stirring to dissolve completely. *Don't* simmer the gelatin or the high heat will render it inactive. Just whisk it in really well. The residual heat of the milk is adequate to activate and dissolve the gelatin.

Strain the milk through a fine-meshed sieve into a medium bowl and set it in a larger bowl of ice water to cool it down quickly. Mix in the cream cheese and vanilla until thoroughly blended and smooth. If you have trouble completely stirring in the cream cheese without lumps, blend with an immersion blender once

the mixture has cooled. Set aside in the refrigerator.

For the butterscotch cake, put the butter chunks in a pot over medium heat. Swirl the pot around as the butter melts and foams. Cook the butter gently for 5 minutes, until it is a brown-amber color and smells nutty. Strain the brown butter to remove any bits and cool to room temperature; chill the brown butter in the refrigerator to solidify. You should have about 9 ounces of brown butter (1 cup plus 2 tablespoons).

Preheat the oven to 375°F. Coat a 9 × 13–inch baking dish with nonstick spray.

Sift the flour, baking powder, baking soda, and salt into a medium bowl. In another large bowl, cream the brown sugar and the 9 ounces of prepared brown butter, for 3 to 4 minutes, until very light and creamy. Mix in the eggs, yolks, and vanilla in 2 additions, beating very well each time to blend.

Add the dry ingredients to the egg mixture, stirring just to combine—don't overwork or the batter can become tough. Stir in the buttermilk and incorporate into a smooth batter. Pour into the prepared pan and smooth with a spatula. Bake for 20 to 25 minutes, until the cake is springy to the touch and medium brown in color.

To make the caramel apples, in a sauté pan over medium-low flame, combine the sugar with 2 tablespoons of water; it should look like wet sand. Cook until the sugar melts and begins to caramelize into a syrup, about 5 minutes. Continue to cook until the sugar begins to boil and takes on a medium amber color,

about 3 minutes more. Be careful, the sugar is *really* hot at this point. Stir in the butter, which will foam a little bit, and continue to cook for 2 minutes, until combined. Once the sugar and butter become a caramel sauce, mix in the cream. When the bubbling has subsided, put in the sliced apples in a rough single layer; season with the cinnamon and salt. Stir occasionally for 6 to 7 minutes, until the apples are fork-tender. Remove from the heat, cover, and hold warm until you are ready to serve.

To prepare the crumble topping, preheat the oven to 350°F. Line a baking sheet with parchment paper.

Put all the ingredients in a medium mixing bowl. Using your hands, crumble the ingredients together to combine until the butter is absorbed. You want a medium-size crumb, not a big wad of dough. Sprinkle the crumbs on the prepared pan and bake for 6 to 7 minutes, so that the crumble is toasted but not hard. Stir the crumbs halfway through baking so that they stay broken up. Cool to room temperature. The crisp topping may be stored in an airtight plastic container for 2 to 3 days.

To assemble the dessert, spoon or pipe the cheesecake cream onto the cooled cake, spread with an offset spatula to cover evenly, and spoon some warm caramel apples on top. Sprinkle the final layer with the toasted crisp topping. Pat down to compress the layers for easy cutting. Cut straight down the center, then make 3 cuts across to yield 8 pieces. Serve with ice cream or whipped cream.

LEVER HOUSE FAVORITE BIRTHDAY CAKE MAKES 1 (9-INCH) CAKE

This chocolate-lover's cake is not on the menu but is a special order at Lever House for celebrations. When people request a birthday cake at the Lever House, this is the hands-down favorite. I inherited the devil's food recipe from an old chef of mine, the late Heather Ho, and have never found one quite as delicious and moist. Don't let the mayonnaise scare you—after all, what is mayo besides eggs and oil? If you want to simplify the process, skip the whipped ganache and just fill and ice the cake with the buttercream.

DEVIL'S FOOD CAKE

1¾ cups cocoa powder

1½ cups boiling water

3½ cups all-purpose flour

1¼ teaspoons baking powder

1 teaspoon baking soda

½ teaspoon salt

¾ cup mayonnaise

3½ cups light brown sugar, lightly packed

3 large eggs

1 tablespoon natural vanilla extract

1½ cups buttermilk

MILK CHOCOLATE GANACHE

2 cups heavy cream

7 ounces milk chocolate, chopped

BRITTLE CRUNCH

1 tablespoon light corn syrup

2 cups granulated sugar

2½ tablespoons unsalted butter

BUTTERCREAM

7 large egg yolks

½ cup light corn syrup

¾ cup granulated sugar

1 tablespoon natural vanilla extract

2 cups (4 sticks) unsalted butter, at room temperature and cut into chunks

6 ounces good-quality bittersweet chocolate, such as Valrhona or Scharffen Berger, melted

To make the devil's food cake, preheat the oven to 375°F.

Coat three 9-inch round cake pans with non-stick cooking spray and dust very lightly with flour. Cut rounds of parchment paper, stick them to the bottom of the pans, and spray the parchment lightly.

Put the cocoa powder in a bowl and pour the boiling water over it; don't measure out the water before it has boiled or some will evaporate, leaving the finished cake dry. Whisk the cocoa sauce very well, until it is perfectly smooth and glossy, making sure there are no pockets of undissolved cocoa. Cover loosely with plastic and set aside.

Sift together twice the flour, baking powder, baking soda, and salt; set aside.

Put the mayonnaise, brown sugar, eggs, and vanilla in the bowl of a standing electric mixer fitted with a paddle attachment, or use a hand-held electric beater. Beat on medium speed until fluffy, light, and well homogenized, about 4 minutes.

Add the sifted dry ingredients into the creamed mixture and mix to combine. Pour the buttermilk into the batter and continue to mix to incorporate. Make sure you don't see any lumps, as those will show up in the finished cake. Fold in the dissolved cocoa by hand until it is completely combined.

Pour the batter into the prepared pans, smooth out the tops with a spatula, and tap the pans lightly to knock out the air and level them; the pans should be two-thirds full. Place the pans on the middle rack of the oven and bake for 15 to 20 minutes, until the cake is springy and fairly firm to the touch and just starting to separate from the sides of the pans. Cool for about 10 minutes. Loosen the cakes from the sides of the pans by running a thin metal spatula around the inside rims, then turn out the cakes onto a platter or wire rack. Peel off the parchment and let the cakes cool for at least 1 hour.

To make the ganache, in a small saucepan over low heat, scald the cream. Put the chopped chocolate in a medium mixing bowl. Slowly add the hot cream to the chocolate in a stream, stirring constantly to slowly melt the chocolate. Set aside to cool completely.

To make the brittle crunch, in a heavy saucepan over medium-high heat, combine the corn syrup, sugar, and butter. Cook until the sugar has melted and caramelizes to a medium amber color, about 3 minutes.

Line a baking sheet with a Silpat or lightly brush it with oil. Carefully pour the hot sugar mixture onto the prepared baking sheet and set aside to get completely hard. After it firms up, grind it to a fine powder in the food processor. Store in a covered, airtight container.

To make the buttercream, put the egg yolks in the bowl of a standing electric mixer fitted with a wire whip attachment, or use a hand-held electric beater. Beat on medium-high speed until the yolks double in volume and are thick and yellow.

Put the corn syrup and sugar in a small pot and stir to combine. Bring to a full rolling boil and carefully pour over the whipped yolks. Keep whipping in order to cool slightly. Add the vanilla and mix in. With the mixer running, add the butter in small pieces, allowing it to incorporate after each addition. After all the butter is in, pour in the melted chocolate and combine thoroughly. The buttercream will be soft at this stage. Set the frosting in the refrigerator to firm up to a spreadable consistency. It can be chilled slightly and used, or stored chilled for several days in airtight containers. It can also be frozen for several months.

To assemble the cake, put a cardboard cake round or plate on a lazy Susan so it is easier to turn and frost the cake. Lay 1 cake layer on the cardboard. Put the ganache in the bowl of an electric mixer and whip as for whipped cream. With a metal spatula, spread about 1/2 cup of the ganache evenly on top of the base. Sprinkle with a handful of the brittle dust. Carefully place a cake layer on top, and repeat with the ganache and the brittle. Put the third cake on top. Chill to set. (The cake can also be frozen overnight.)

When the cake is set, frost it with the buttercream. If the buttercream has been sitting in the refrigerator for hours, it should be whipped in a mixer to an easily spreadable consistency. Frost the top and sides of the cake thoroughly. Refrigerate the cake for a few minutes (or as long as several hours) before decorating or cutting.

CHOCOLATE CHEESECAKE SERVES 8 TO 10

It seems like this cheesecake's chocolate crust can be made from almost anything. You can buy graham crackers or chocolate wafers from the grocery store, grind them in the food processor, and add some melted butter to make the crust. You could also use any kind of stale chocolate cake or cookie this way. For a store-bought chocolate wafer crust, you will need a roughly 9-ounce box of cookies, crushed and moistened with 2 to 3 tablespoons of melted butter.

CHOCOLATE CRUST

6 tablespoons unsalted butter, cut in chunks

¼ cup sugar

¾ cup all-purpose flour

¼ cup cocoa powder

½ teaspoon salt

2 to 3 tablespoons melted unsalted butter

CHOCOLATE CHEESECAKE

1 cup heavy cream

9 ounces good-quality bittersweet chocolate, such as Valrhona or Scharffen Berger, coarsely chopped (about 2 cups)

22 ounces (2¾ 8-ounce packages) cream cheese, at room temperature

⅔ cup sugar

4 large eggs

1 teaspoon natural vanilla extract

To prepare the crust, preheat the oven to 375°F. Lightly coat the bottom and sides of an 8-inch springform pan with nonstick cooking spray. Line a sheet pan with a Silpat or parchment paper. It is easiest to use a Silpat, since you will be crumbling and mixing the crust as it bakes, and parchment can tear if you get too rough.

Cream together the butter and sugar until very light and well combined. Add the flour, cocoa powder, and salt and mix just to combine and hold loosely together. Spoon the dough in teaspoon-size chunks onto the lined

pan. Bake for 10 minutes, or until the dough starts to set.

Remove the dough from the oven and, using a dry dishcloth, bench knife, or slotted spoon, crumble the mixture, breaking up whatever has baked together. You are attempting to make crumbs rather than baked dough. Return the pieces of dough to the oven, and continue to crumble every 6 to 7 minutes, until it is baked very dry. Don't worry if the pieces are not fine enough. You can grind the crumbs again in a food processor or crush them with a rolling pin once they have cooled.

When the dough is cooled and crushed, combine it with enough melted butter just to dampen the crumbs and to allow the crust to hold together loosely. Pat the crumbs into the prepared springform pan.

To make the cheesecake filling, preheat the oven to 350°F.

In a small saucepan, scald the cream. Put the chopped chocolate in a medium mixing bowl. Slowly add the hot cream in a stream, stirring constantly to melt the chocolate.

Put the cream cheese in the bowl of a standing electric mixer fitted with a paddle attachment, or use a hand-held electric beater. Turn the mixer on medium-high speed and beat the cream cheese until it is very smooth and lump free. Stop the machine periodically to scrape the cream cheese off the paddle and the sides of the bowl. Beat in the sugar, which

should help to lighten the mixture and make it creamy. Add the eggs, one at a time, and then the vanilla, beating well after each addition. Finally, add the melted chocolate and mix to combine completely.

Pour the filling into the crust-lined pan and tap the pan lightly on the counter to knock out some of the air bubbles. Smooth the surface with a spatula to even it out.

To bake the cake in a water bath, set the cheesecake pan on a large piece of aluminum foil and fold up the sides around the pan; the foil will keep the water from seeping into the cheesecake from the bottom of the bath. Set the cake pan in a larger roasting pan. Pour very hot (not boiling) water into the roasting pan until the water is about halfway up the sides of the cake pan. Cover the entire roasting pan tightly with foil. Steam the cake for about 55 minutes, until it is set on the sides but still jiggles slightly in the center. It will firm up after chilling.

Carefully, remove the cheesecake from the water bath and cool to room temperature. Chill in the refrigerator, loosely covered, for at least 4 hours.

Loosen the cheesecake from the sides of the pan by running a thin metal spatula around the inside rim of the ring. Unmold and transfer to a cake plate. Slice the cheesecake with a thin, nonserrated knife that has been dipped in hot water and wiped dry after each cut.

Lever House will always have a warm cookie plate on the menu, and it's perfect for sharing. Although we change the cookies and drink according to our whim and the seasons, the warm cookies have been a popular dessert since we opened. The first menu we did featured the cookies accompanied by a little shot glass filled with this malted shake; people went nuts for it and requested rounds for the whole table. Cookies and ice cream are a craving that satisfies and appeals to all ages. The four varieties of cookies are also a match for Hot Chocolate (page 206). For all cookies except the peanut butter, err on the side of *under-baking* to ensure that they come out soft in the center and crispy just on the edges.

peanut butter and jelly cookies

MAKES 40 COOKIES (20 SANDWICHES)

COOKIE DOUGH

½ cup (1 stick) unsalted butter, cut in chunks

⅓ cup smooth peanut butter

½ cup plus 2 tablespoons confectioners' sugar

1 large egg

1 large egg yolk

1¼ teaspoons natural vanilla extract

2¼ cups all-purpose flour

¼ teaspoon baking powder

¼ teaspoon salt

Sugar in the raw, for dusting

PEANUT BUTTER AND JELLY FILLING

½ cup smooth peanut butter

½ cup jam (such as raspberry or strawberry)

2 teaspoons granulated sugar

To make the dough, put the butter, peanut butter, and confectioners' sugar in the bowl of a standing electric mixer fitted with a paddle attachment, or use a hand-held electric beater. Cream the mixture together until it's very light, fluffy, and well combined, probably 4 to 5 minutes. Using a rubber spatula, scrape down the sides of the bowl a couple of times during this process. Add the egg, yolk, and vanilla and beat with the butter mixture to lighten.

In a separate bowl, combine the flour, baking powder, and salt. Add them to the creamed mixture in 2 additions, beating both times just to combine. Do not overbeat the dough or it will become tough.

Divide the dough in half and flatten both pieces into a rectangle, about 8 × 3 inches. Roll out each rectangle separately between sheets of parchment paper to about ⅛ inch thick. Chill the dough for about 1 hour before cutting it into cookies.

Preheat the oven to 375°F. Line 2 cookie sheets with parchment paper.

When the dough is chilled, peel off the pieces of parchment paper and cut the dough into desired shapes using a knife or cookie cutter. At the restaurant we use 2-inch squares, and cut small circles into half of the squares to allow a window for the filling to show in the finished cookies. Place the cut cookies on the prepared baking sheets about 1 inch apart. Sprinkle the surface of the cookies with sugar in the raw. Bake for about 10 minutes, until light brown and firm to the touch. Cool on a rack completely before sandwiching them with the peanut butter and jelly filling. It's okay to roll up the scraps and knock out another batch, although they may be a little tough.

To make the filling, put the peanut butter, jam, and sugar in the bowl of a standing electric mixer fitted with a paddle attachment, or use a hand-held electric beater. Beat well to combine. Spread the filling on the bottom half of the cookies and top with another cookie to make a sandwich (if you have opted to cut holes in half of them, this one should be on the top). Make sure the sugared side of each cookie faces out. Serve warm.

snickerdoodles (cinnamon-sugar cookies)

MAKES 20 COOKIES (ABOUT 3 INCHES IN DIAMETER)

3 tablespoons plus 2 teaspoons cinnamon

2½ cups sugar

1 cup (2 sticks) unsalted butter, at room temperature

2 tablespoons light corn syrup

2 large eggs

3½ cups all-purpose flour

1½ teaspoons baking soda

1 teaspoon baking powder

¼ teaspoon salt

In a small bowl, stir together 3 tablespoons of cinnamon and ½ cup of sugar; set aside.

Put the butter, 2 cups sugar, and corn syrup in the bowl of a standing electric mixer fitted with a paddle attachment, or use a hand-held electric beater. Beat on medium speed until fluffy and light. Beat in the eggs, 1 at a time.

In a separate bowl, combine the flour, the remaining 2 teaspoons cinnamon, baking soda, baking powder, and salt. Add the dry ingredients to the creamed mixture in 2 additions, beating both times just to combine. Do not overbeat or the dough will become tough.

Preheat the oven to 375°F. Line 2 baking sheets with parchment paper.

Using your palms, roll the dough into 2-inch balls, about the size of a golf ball, then roll them in the cinnamon-sugar to coat. Place on the prepared baking sheets about 2 inches apart. Bake until the cookies are just set on the edges but still moist, about 9 minutes. Cool on a rack for 5 minutes and serve warm.

double chocolate cookies

MAKES 3½ DOZEN

¼ cup (½ stick) unsalted butter, cut in chunks

4 ounces unsweetened chocolate, chopped

12 ounces good-quality bittersweet chocolate,
   such as Valrhona or Scharffen Berger,
   chopped

4 large eggs

1⅔ cups sugar

1 teaspoon natural vanilla extract

1 teaspoon strongly brewed coffee
   or coffee extract

½ cup all-purpose flour

1¼ teaspoons baking powder

¼ teaspoon salt

10 ounces good-quality chopped milk
   chocolate or chocolate chips

1 cup toasted, chopped walnuts

To create a double boiler, bring a pot of water to a simmer over medium-low heat. Combine the butter and the unsweetened and bittersweet chocolates in a metal or glass heat-resistant bowl and set over the simmering water, without letting the bottom touch. Stir until melted and smooth. Set aside to cool.

Put the eggs and sugar in the bowl of a standing electric mixer fitted with a wire whip attachment, or use a hand-held electric beater. Beat on medium speed until fluffy and light. Add the vanilla and coffee. Pour in the melted chocolate and continue to whip until well combined. Mix the flour, baking powder, and salt into the batter. Fold in the chips and nuts.

Transfer the batter into a clean bowl. It will be too sticky to form into cookies now, but let it stand at room temperature for about 30 minutes and it will become easier to handle.

Preheat the oven to 350°F. Line 2 baking sheets with parchment paper.

Scoop the dough by the heaping tablespoon and put on the prepared baking sheets about 1 inch apart. Bake until the cookies are just set but still moist, about 10 minutes. Cool on a rack for 5 minutes and serve warm.

best chocolate chip cookies

MAKES 3 DOZEN

1 cup (2 sticks) unsalted butter, at room
   temperature and cut in chunks

⅔ cup granulated sugar

1¼ cups dark brown sugar, lightly packed

3 tablespoons light corn syrup

2 large eggs

1 teaspoon natural vanilla extract

3⅓ cups all-purpose flour

1 teaspoon baking soda

1 teaspoon salt

10 ounces good-quality bittersweet chocolate,
   such as Valrhona or Scharffen Berger,
   coarsely chopped

4 ounces good-quality milk chocolate, such as
   Valrhona or Scharffen Berger, chopped

Put the butter, sugars, and corn syrup in the bowl of a standing electric mixer fitted with a paddle attachment, or use a hand-held electric beater. Beat on medium speed until fluffy and light, about 5 minutes. Beat in the eggs, 1 at a time, combining well after each addition. Stir in the vanilla.

In a separate bowl, combine the flour, baking soda, and salt. Add the dry ingredients to the creamed mixture in 2 additions, beating both times just to combine. Do not overbeat the dry ingredients or the cookie dough will become tough. Fold in the chopped chocolates and mix until well distributed.

Preheat the oven to 375°F. Line 2 baking sheets with parchment paper.

Using your palms, roll the dough into 2-inch balls, about the size of a golf ball. Place the balls on the prepared baking sheets about 2 inches apart. Bake until the cookies are just set on the edges but still fairly gooey in the center, about 9 minutes. Cool on a rack for 5 minutes and serve warm.

black-and-white malted shake

SERVES 4 TO 6

6 large scoops Malted Vanilla Ice Cream
   (recipe follows)

1 quart milk

½ cup chocolate sauce or syrup

2 tablespoons malt powder or liquid malt

1 tablespoon natural vanilla extract

To make the malteds, put all the ingredients in a blender and mix to the desired consistency. Pour into chilled glasses and serve with the cookie plate.

malted vanilla ice cream

MAKES 1 QUART

2$\frac{1}{2}$ cups milk

1$\frac{1}{2}$ cups heavy cream

1 cup sugar

1 vanilla bean

8 large egg yolks (about $\frac{3}{4}$ cup)

1 cup plus 3 tablespoons malted milk powder

1 teaspoon natural vanilla extract

In a large pot over medium heat, combine the milk, cream, and sugar. Scrape out the seeds of the vanilla bean and add them and the pod to the milk mixture. Heat gently until the sugar is dissolved, about 5 minutes.

In a large bowl, whisk together the yolks and malt powder. Using a large ladle or measuring cup, temper the yolks by gradually whisking half of the hot vanilla milk into the yolk mixture. Do not add the hot milk too quickly or the eggs will cook and begin to scramble.

Add the eggs back into the pot of remaining milk and whisk constantly over medium heat, just until the custard is thick enough to coat the back of a spoon, about 5 minutes. Pass the custard through a fine-meshed strainer into a large container. Chill completely in a sink full of ice, stirring here and there; this should take about $\frac{1}{2}$ hour. Mix in the vanilla.

Churn the custard in an ice cream maker according to manufacturer's directions. When done, the ice cream will be the consistency of soft serve. To harden it fully, freeze it in a covered plastic container.

CRANBERRY-PECAN TART WITH MAPLE ICE CREAM

This takes pecan pie to another level. A perfect holiday-time dessert, with or without the ice cream, this is one of the simplest desserts to make. It is always featured during the holidays on the Lever House Thanksgiving and Christmas menus. Fresh or frozen cranberries can be used.

TART PASTRY

14 tablespoons (1¾ sticks) unsalted butter, cold and cut into chunks

⅔ cup confectioners' sugar

1 large egg

2 cups plus 2 tablespoons all-purpose flour

¾ cup almond flour

CRANBERRY-PECAN FILLING

1 cup granulated sugar

1¼ cups heavy cream

2 cups fresh cranberries

1 teaspoon salt

9 ounces pecans, toasted and coarsely chopped (about 2½ cups)

Maple Ice Cream (recipe follows)

Put the butter and confectioners' sugar in the bowl of a standing electric mixer fitted with a paddle attachment, or use a hand-held electric beater. Cream them together until well combined and soft, like shortbread cookie dough. Add the egg and, once incorporated, the flours; mix just to combine. Gather the dough in a ball and wrap in plastic to chill for about 30 minutes, until firm.

Using a floured rolling pin, roll the dough out on a lightly floured surface to a 12-inch circle about ¼ inch thick. Carefully lay it inside a 10 ½-inch tart pan with a removable bottom, pressing the edges evenly into the sides of the ring. Trim off any excess hanging dough. Chill for at least 30 minutes.

Preheat the oven to 350°F.

Prick the tart shell all over with the tines of a fork. Bake until almost completely cooked, about 15 minutes. While the shell is baking, make the filling.

To prepare the filling, start by making caramel. In a pot, combine the sugar with 2 tablespoons of water; heat over a medium-low flame; it should look like wet sand. Cook until the sugar melts and begins to caramelize into a syrup, about 5 to 7 minutes. Continue to cook until the sugar begins to boil and takes on a medium amber color; be careful, the sugar is *really* hot at this point. Remove from the heat and slowly add the cream, a bit at a time, to the hot syrup. It will sputter a bit, so stand back as you pour. When all the bubbling has died down, put the pot back on the burner, and bring the mixture to a boil. This will bring together the caramel.

Remove the caramel from the heat and mix in the cranberries, salt, and pecans, making sure to distribute the ingredients evenly through the caramel.

Ladle the filling into the prepared tart shell and smooth out the top. Put the tart pan on a sheet pan so it will be easier to move in and out of the oven. Bake for about 20 to 25 minutes, until the filling has set slightly and the cranberries have begun to pop. Serve the tart warm topped with ice cream.

maple ice cream

MAKES ABOUT 1 QUART

1¾ cups maple syrup

1 cup heavy cream

3 cups milk

1 cup large egg yolks (1 dozen eggs)

2 tablespoons sugar

1 teaspoon natural vanilla extract

½ teaspoon salt

In a heavy saucepot, bring the maple syrup to a controlled boil over medium-high heat. Reduce the heat and simmer until the syrup is reduced by a third, about 10 minutes. The syrup should have caramelized and taken on some color. Remove from the heat and slowly add the cream, a bit at a time, to the hot syrup. It will sputter a bit, so stand back as you pour. When all the bubbling has died down, put the pot back on the burner, and bring the mixture to a boil. This will bring together the mixture. Pour the maple syrup cream into a large heat-resistant bowl.

To make the custard, return the same pot to the stove, pour in the milk, and scald over medium heat.

In a large bowl, whisk together the yolks and sugar. Using a large ladle or measuring cup, temper the yolks by gradually whisking half of the hot milk into the yolk-and-sugar mixture. Do not add the hot milk too quickly or the eggs will cook and begin to scramble.

Add the tempered eggs back into the pot of remaining milk and stir constantly over medium heat, just until the custard is thick enough to coat the back of a spoon, about 5 minutes. Pass the custard through a fine-meshed strainer into the maple syrup mixture, whisking to blend. Chill completely in a sink full of ice, stirring here and there; this should take about ½ hour. Mix in the vanilla and salt.

Churn the custard in an ice cream maker according to the manufacturer's directions. When done, the ice cream will be the consistency of soft serve. To harden the ice cream fully, freeze it in a covered plastic container.

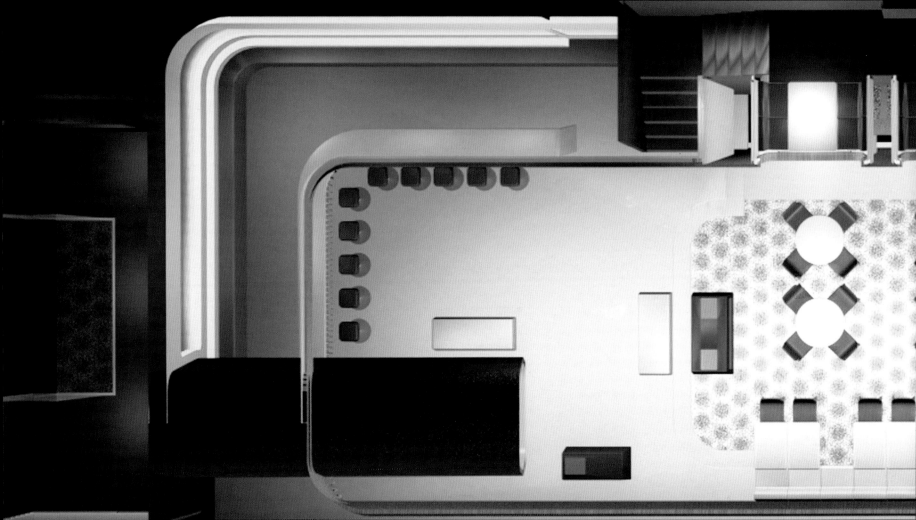

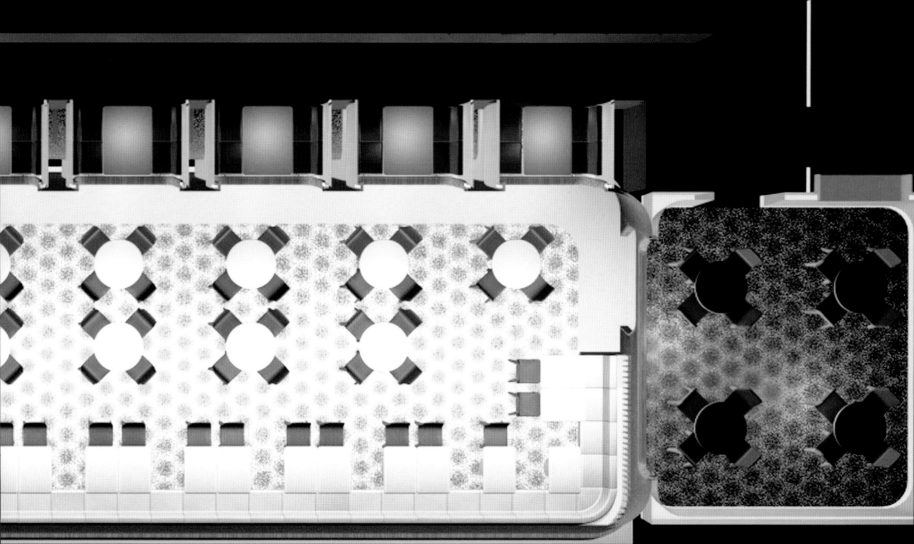

People think Lever House is stuffy Park Avenue dining, but this homey dessert sells out every time it is on the menu. These doughnuts are not dense; they are light as a feather and fantastic for dunking. The addition of the mashed potatoes is inspired by a midwestern state-fair idea that is not uncommon to see in Mom and Pop recipes. The black pepper adds a little spice and dimension to the hot chocolate. Add 2 to 4 tablespoons brandy, crème de menthe, or other liqueur of your choice, if you are over twenty-one, of course.

DOUGHNUTS

¼ cup (½ stick) unsalted butter, at room temperature

¼ cup granulated sugar

¼ cup mashed potato (½ Idaho potato, boiled and mashed)

1⅓ cups milk

1 vanilla bean

1 tablespoon fresh yeast, or 1 (¼-ounce) package of active dry yeast

¼ cup warm water

1 large egg

¼ teaspoon natural vanilla extract

3½ cups all-purpose flour

½ teaspoon baking powder

1½ teaspoons salt

Canola oil, for oiling the bowl and deep-frying

Confectioners' sugar or cinnamon-sugar, for dusting

HOT CHOCOLATE

2 cups milk

1 cup heavy cream

¼ cup light brown sugar, lightly packed

1 cinnamon stick, smashed

Pinch of freshly ground black pepper

4 ounces good-quality bittersweet chocolate, such as Valrhona or Scharffen Berger, coarsely chopped

¼ teaspoon salt

To make the doughnuts, in a large bowl, combine the butter, sugar, and mashed potato. In a small pot over medium-low heat, warm the milk. Scrape out the seeds of the vanilla bean and add them and the pod to the milk. Bring the milk to a brief simmer to infuse with the vanilla; do not boil or it can overflow. Remove the pod from the pot and pour the hot vanilla milk over the butter mixture, stirring well to combine. Set aside to cool to room temperature.

Meanwhile, bloom the yeast and warm water in the bowl of a standing electric mixer fitted with a paddle attachment. Let them stand for 10 minutes, until foam appears, which indicates that the yeast is active.

Stir the egg and vanilla extract into the milk mixture. Pour everything over the yeast in the mixer and turn it on low speed. With the mixer running, add the flour, baking powder, and salt a little at a time to incorporate. When the dough starts to come together, increase the speed to medium and continue to mix for 6 to 7 minutes to knead the dough, which should be smooth, supple, and sticky to the touch.

Place the dough in a lightly oiled bowl, turning to coat all sides. Cover loosely with a towel or plastic wrap, and put in a warm place to allow the dough to rise, about 1 hour.

Using a floured rolling pin, roll the dough out on a lightly floured surface to about ¾ inch thick. Transfer the dough to a sheet pan lined with parchment and coated with nonstick spray; cover and chill in the refrigerator to proof for at least 30 minutes and up to 3 or 4 hours.

Cut out the doughnuts using a floured dough-nut cutter, or a 3-inch biscuit cutter (use a smaller ring to cut out the hole in the center). Place the doughnuts and doughnut holes on a baking sheet lined with parchment paper, cover, and chill in the refrigerator while heating the oil.

Heat 3 inches of canola oil to 375°F. in an electric fryer or deep saucepan. (Check the temperature with an instant-read thermometer or sprinkle some flour in the hot oil; if it sizzles, the oil is ready.)

Slip the doughnuts in the hot oil in batches and fry until golden, about 2 minutes per side, turning over with a slotted spoon or chopsticks so they cook evenly.

Carefully remove the doughnuts to a plate lined with paper towels to drain. Dust with con-fectioners' or cinnamon-sugar while still hot.

To make the hot chocolate, in a medium pot over medium heat, combine the milk, cream, and brown sugar. Stir with a wooden spoon to dissolve the sugar. Add the cinnamon and pep-per. Heat and stir to infuse the flavors until the milk just begins to boil. Pass the liquid through a fine strainer to remove the solids.

Put the chopped chocolate in a mixing bowl. Slowly add the flavored milk mixture to the chocolate in a stream, stirring constantly to slowly melt the chocolate. If you rush this step, the chocolate can break and will not have a smooth, glossy finish. Continue to add the milk until it is all combined. Season the hot choco-late with the salt and serve immediately, or put in a thermos for future pleasure.

CHOCOLATE-MINT ICE BOX CAKE WITH MINT CHIP ICE CREAM SERVES 8 TO 10

This is the best-selling Lever House dessert ever. The chocolate-mint combo is the ultimate expression of everyone's favorite Girl Scout cookie.

We realize that this looks like a daunting recipe, and it is somewhat time consuming. The good news is that if you make all the components ahead of time, you can assemble it fairly quickly. At the restaurant, the chocolate mousse, mint mousse, and meringue topping are piped out of pastry bags for easy cleanup. Disposable pastry bags are readily available, or the old trick of cutting off the corner of a resealable plastic bag works in a pinch. If all else fails, simply spread the mousses and meringue on the cake with an offset spatula.

Chocolate Crust (page 197)

GANACHE
½ cup heavy cream
4 ounces good-quality bittersweet chocolate, such as Valrhona or Scharffen Berger, coarsely chopped

MINT MOUSSE
5 large egg yolks
¾ cup sugar
¼ cup water
6 gelatin sheets or 1½ (¼-ounce) envelopes powdered unflavored gelatin
2 tablespoons crème de menthe (white or green)
2 teaspoons natural mint extract
2 cups heavy cream

CHOCOLATE MOUSSE
9 ounces good-quality bittersweet chocolate, such as Valrhona or Scharffen Berger, coarsely chopped (about 2 cups)
6 tablespoons unsalted butter, at room temperature and cut in chunks
7 ounces heavy cream
5 large eggs, separated
3 tablespoons sugar

MERINGUE
3 large egg whites (about 4½ ounces)
1½ cups sugar

Mint Chip Ice Cream (recipe follows)

Bake the crust for about 8 minutes, just to set and dry. When baked, set aside while you make the rest of the cake layers.

To make the ganache, in a small saucepan over low heat, scald the cream. Put the chocolate in a mixing bowl. Slowly add the hot cream to the chocolate in a stream, stirring constantly to melt the chocolate. Pour the warm ganache in an even layer over the prepared crust. Refrigerate the whole crust to set.

To prepare the mint mousse, put the egg yolks in the bowl of a standing electric mixer fitted with a paddle attachment, or use a hand-held electric beater. Whip the yolks on medium-high speed until thick and pale yellow.

In a small saucepan over medium heat, combine the sugar and the water. Put a candy thermometer in the pot and bring the mixture to a boil. You want to bring the sugar to the softball stage, or 240°F. Pull the sugar from the heat and pour over the whipping yolks. Keep the machine on.

Soak the gelatin sheets in cool water for 2 minutes to soften, then remove and squeeze out the excess water (if using powdered gelatin, soak it in ¼ cup cool water for 3 minutes).

Place the crème de menthe and mint extract in a small saucepan and warm over low heat, until warm to the touch. Remove from the heat. Add the bloomed gelatin to the warm mint liquid and whisk very well until the gelatin is completely dissolved. Pour this mixture into the whipped eggs. Allow the egg mixture to cool completely.

Whip the cream to soft peaks and fold it into the cooled egg mixture to lighten it up. Refrigerate the mint mousse to set.

To make the chocolate mousse, melt the chocolate over a double boiler. Remove from the heat. Add the softened butter and stir to combine until smooth. In a small saucepan over medium heat, scald the cream. Pour it over the chocolate butter and whisk it all together until smooth and glossy.

Put the egg yolks and half of the sugar in the bowl of a standing electric mixer fitted with a wire whip attachment, or use a hand-held electric beater. Whip the yolks on medium-high speed until they are thick and pale yellow. Fold the yolks into the chocolate mixture.

In a clean bowl, whip the whites until they become opaquely frothy. Add the remaining half of the sugar in a slow, steady stream. Continue whipping until the whites hold soft peaks. Fold these carefully into the chocolate mixture and place in the refrigerator.

To prepare the meringue, bring a pot of water to a simmer over medium-low heat. In a metal or glass heat-resistant bowl, combine the egg whites and the sugar and whisk until smooth. Set the bowl over the simmering water, without letting the bottom touch. Whisk the mixture well, making sure to incorporate the sugar on the sides of the bowl. When the mixture is hot to the touch and when you cannot feel any sugar grains if you dip your finger in, the meringue is ready to transfer to the mixer. Whip the meringue on high speed until cool

and glossy, probably 3 to 4 minutes. The fluffy whites should be opaque and have stiff peaks. Transfer the meringue to a pastry bag fitted with a large, plain tip and set it in the refrigerator until the cake is assembled.

To assemble, put the mint mousse and chocolate mousse in 2 separate pastry bags fitted with a large round tip (or no tip at all). Pipe the mint mousse over the ganache crust in an even, uniform layer. Pipe the chocolate mousse over the mint mousse until you've reached the top of the ring of the pan. Pipe the meringue over the top of the cake in whimsical swirls (try to avoid bringing it completely to the outer edge as it makes unmolding more difficult). Wrap the cake loosely in plastic wrap and place in the freezer for at least 4 hours and as long as 3 days.

To serve, allow the cake to come to room temperature for about 15 minutes. Unmold the springform and then torch the meringue until it is a deep brown. It is now ready to present and slice. Serve with ice cream.

mint chip ice cream

MAKES 1 QUART

2½ cups milk

1½ cups heavy cream

1 vanilla bean

8 sprigs fresh peppermint, leaves and stems, coarsely chopped

1 cup egg yolks (1 dozen large eggs)

1 cup sugar

1 tablespoon crème de menthe

½ tablespoon natural mint extract

¾ cup finely chopped good-quality bittersweet chocolate, such as Valrhona or Scharffen Berger

Combine the milk and cream in a pot. Scrape out the seeds of the vanilla bean and add them to the milk mixture; put the pod in there, too, for extra flavor. Add the peppermint and bring to a boil over medium heat. Remove from the heat and allow to steep for 1 hour to infuse the vanilla and mint flavors into the milk mixture. Return the milk mixture to a boil.

In a large bowl, whisk together the yolks and sugar. Using a large ladle or measuring cup, temper the yolks by gradually whisking half of the hot milk into the yolk-and-sugar mixture. Do not add the hot milk too quickly or the eggs will cook and begin to scramble.

Add the tempered eggs back into the pot of remaining milk and whisk constantly over medium heat, just until the custard is thick enough to coat the back of a spoon, about 5 minutes. Pass the custard through a fine-meshed strainer into a large container. Chill completely in a sink full of ice, stirring here and there; this should take about ½ hour. Mix in the crème de menthe and mint extract.

Churn the mixture in an ice cream maker according to the manufacturer's directions. When done, the ice cream will be the consistency of soft serve. Fold in the chopped chocolate and allow the ice cream to freeze fully, until firm, in a covered plastic container.

LEMON MERINGUE–BLUEBERRY PIE SERVES 8 TO 12

This is a great summertime do-ahead dessert and a fun twist on a classic pie. You could substitute any fresh berries from your farmer's market; blackberries or raspberries would work wonderfully, or you could combine several of your favorites.

CRUST
2 cups finely ground graham crackers (about 26 squares)

½ cup (1 stick) melted unsalted butter

1½ tablespoons dark brown sugar

LEMON CURD
6 large eggs

6 large egg yolks (3 whites reserved for meringue)

1 cup granulated sugar

Juice and zest of 8 lemons (about 1 cup of fresh lemon juice)

1 cup (2 sticks) unsalted butter, at room temperature

½ cup heavy cream, whipped

BLUEBERRY COMPOTE
2 pints blueberries, picked through

¼ cup granulated sugar

1 teaspoon freshly squeezed lemon juice

½ teaspoon finely grated lemon zest

Pinch of ground cinnamon

Pinch of salt

2 teaspoons all-purpose flour

MERINGUE
3 large egg whites (about 4½ ounces)

1½ cups granulated sugar

Preheat the oven to 350°F.

To prepare the crumb crust, in a mixing bowl combine the crust ingredients with a fork until evenly moistened. Lightly coat the bottom and sides of a 10-inch springform pan with nonstick cooking spray. Firmly press the crumb mixture over the bottom of the pan, using your fingers or the smooth base; don't line the crumbs up the sides of the pan. Bake for 7 minutes, just to toast and set the crust. Cool while preparing the filling.

To make the lemon curd, create a double boiler: bring a pot of water to a simmer over medium-low heat. In a metal or glass heat-resistant bowl, combine the eggs, yolks, sugar, and zest; whisk to combine loosely. Set the bowl over the simmering water, without letting the bottom touch, and continue to whisk. Stir in the lemon juice. Whisk the lemon curd thoroughly every few moments (it does not have to be constantly attended to), until the curd is very thick and yellow. The curd should pile up on itself. Don't let it boil.

Remove the bowl from the heat and whisk in the butter, a couple of chunks at a time, until melted. Strain through a fine-meshed sieve to remove the zest and make the custard smooth. Put a piece of plastic directly on the surface of the curd to prevent a skin from forming on top. Refrigerate until cold and firm, at least 4 hours.

Put 1 cup of the chilled lemon curd into a mixing bowl and fold in the whipped cream to lighten it up into a mousse; reserve in the refrigerator. Pipe or spread the remaining chilled lemon curd into the prepared, cooled crust. Chill for 1 hour to set while making the blueberry compote.

To prepare the blueberry compote, put 1 pint of blueberries in a small pot over medium heat with the sugar, lemon juice and zest, cinnamon, and salt. Stir gently until the blueberries start to turn dark and release their natural juice. The consistency should remain a bit chunky; don't overcook and dissolve the berries to mush. Remove the pot from the heat and stir in the flour to thicken the compote slightly. Fold in the remaining pint of blueberries and transfer to a bowl to cool.

Using a slotted spoon, spread half of the blueberry compote over the bottom layer of the lemon curd pie. Spread the lemon curd mousse evenly on top of the blueberries to neatly cover the surface of the pie. Chill for at least 1 hour to set. When the top layer of the lemon curd is set, use a slotted spoon to arrange the remaining blueberry compote over the top of the pie, spreading just short of the edges so that you allow some of the lemon to show. Chill while making the meringue.

To prepare the meringue, bring a pot of water to a simmer over medium-low heat. In a metal or glass heat-resistant bowl, combine the egg whites and the sugar and whisk until smooth. Set the bowl over the simmering water, without letting the bottom touch. Whisk the meringue mixture well, making sure to incorporate the sugar on the sides of the bowl. When the mixture is hot to the touch and when you cannot feel any sugar grains if you dip in your finger, the meringue is ready to transfer to the mixer. Whip on high speed until cool and shiny, probably 3 to 4 minutes. The fluffy whites should be opaque and form stiff peaks.

Transfer the meringue to a pastry bag fitted with a large, plain tip. Swirl the meringue over the top of the pie, allowing a small edge that shows both the lemon and the blueberries; avoid piping too thick. Feel free to pipe your own patterns, making the meringue as whimsical or as organized as you like.

Just before serving, hold a kitchen torch 2 inches above the surface to brown the meringue and form a crust, or broil it in the oven for 3 minutes, to toast the meringue on top until golden brown.

SWEET CORN AND PEACH TRIFLE SERVES 8

There's nothing like a slurpy ripe peach and sweet corn in the summer when they are at their peaks—it reminds me of being a kid and our lazy summer dinners before we went back to school. As a grown-up I still love these flavors, but wanted to combine them into a sophisticated plated dessert. The use of a corn puree in a pastry cream may sound unusual, but if you love eating corn on the cob, you should try this recipe to see how nicely it works in a dessert. At the restaurant, we serve this trifle with batter-fried slices of peaches and fresh peach ice cream. This trifle is different from the standard English trifle and it will wow your guests.

CORNMEAL CAKE

6 large egg yolks
¼ cup buttermilk
¾ teaspoon natural vanilla extract
2 ears sweet corn, shucked, kernels cut
    from the cob (about 1 cup)
Juice and finely grated zest of 3 limes
3 cups cake flour
⅓ cup plus 1 tablespoon yellow cornmeal
    or coarse polenta
1½ cups granulated sugar
1 tablespoon plus 1 teaspoon baking powder
¾ teaspoon salt
¾ cup (1½ sticks) unsalted butter, at room
    temperature and cut in chunks
¾ cup milk

CORN PASTRY CREAM

8 ears sweet corn, shucked, kernels cut
    from the cob (about 4 cups)
1½ cups heavy cream
1¼ cups granulated sugar
⅓ cup plus 1 teaspoon cornstarch
1 teaspoon salt, plus additional to taste
7 large egg yolks
3 cups milk
1 vanilla bean, split lengthwise
4 gelatin sheets or 1 (¼-ounce) envelope
    powdered unflavored gelatin
3½ tablespoons unsalted butter, at room
    temperature and cut in chunks

ROASTED PEACH FILLING

5 large ripe peaches, pitted and sliced
    ½ inch thick
¼ cup light brown sugar, lightly packed
2 tablespoons freshly squeezed lime juice
Pinch of ground cinnamon
½ teaspoon salt
¼ teaspoon freshly ground white or black
    pepper

CANDIED CORN KERNELS

½ cup granulated sugar
¼ cup water
½ vanilla bean
2 ears sweet corn, shucked, kernels cut
    from the cob (about 1 cup)

To make the cornmeal cake, preheat the oven to 350°F. Line a baking sheet or jelly roll pan with parchment paper and coat lightly with nonstick cooking spray.

In a bowl, combine the yolks, buttermilk, vanilla, corn, lime zest, and juice; set aside.

Put the flour, cornmeal, sugar, baking powder, and salt in the bowl of a standing electric mixer fitted with a paddle attachment, or use a hand-held electric beater. Mix on low speed for about 10 seconds to combine the ingredients. Add the butter and milk and continue to mix until the ingredients are moistened. Raise the mixer speed up to high and beat until light and smooth, about 2 minutes. Using a rubber spatula, scrape down the sides of the bowl a couple of times during this process.

Add half of the egg-corn mixture to the batter and stir to combine. Again, turn the mixer to high and beat for about 30 seconds. Scrape down the sides again and add the remaining half of the egg-corn mixture to the bowl. Stir to combine. Turn the mixer on high and beat well, about 30 seconds.

Spread the cake into the prepared pan and place in the center of the oven. Bake for 20 to 25 minutes, until the cake is lightly colored on the edges. Set aside to allow to cool in the pan.

To make the corn pastry cream, first make the corn puree: Place the corn kernels in a pot with 1 cup of the heavy cream and cook over medium heat just to a boil. (Reserve the remaining cream to whip for the trifle.) Turn down the heat and simmer the corn for 3 to 4 minutes; remove from heat and cool slightly. Transfer the contents of the pot to a blender. Blend the mixture as smooth as possible (alternatively, you can use an immersion blender directly in the pot). You should have about 3 cups. Cover the corn puree with plastic to keep it from drying out and set aside.

In a large bowl, sift together the sugar, cornstarch, and the teaspoon of salt. Add the yolks and whisk into the dry ingredients until they are well combined. Add the corn puree and stir.

Pour the milk into a pot over medium heat. Scrape out the seeds of the vanilla bean and add them to the milk; put the pod in there, too, for extra flavor. Bring the milk to a brief boil.

Temper the yolks by gradually whisking half of the hot vanilla milk into the yolk-and-corn mixture. Do not add the hot milk too quickly or the eggs will cook and begin to scramble. Add the tempered eggs back into the pot of remaining milk and whisk constantly over medium-low heat until the mixture starts to boil. Once it boils, turn the heat down slightly and continue whisking for 30 seconds.

Soak the gelatin sheets in cool water for 2 minutes to soften, then remove and squeeze out the excess water (if using powdered gelatin, soak it in 4 tablespoons cool water for 3 minutes).

Add the bloomed gelatin to the hot milk-and-corn mixture off the stove, stirring to dissolve completely. *Don't* simmer the gelatin or the high heat will render it inactive. Just whisk it in really well. The residual heat of the milk is perfectly adequate to activate and dissolve the gelatin.

Strain the milk through a fine-meshed sieve into a bowl and put in a larger bowl of ice water to cool it down quickly to room temperature. When the milk reaches room temperature, use an immersion blender to add in the butter. Puree the butter until the milk mixture is smooth and silky. Taste and adjust the seasoning. A little bit of salt really makes the corn flavor pronounced.

To make the roasted peach filling, preheat the oven to 350°F.

Place the peaches, brown sugar, lime juice, cinnamon, salt, and pepper in a roasting pan. If necessary, add a small amount of water (or sweet white wine) to coat any dry spots on the bottom of the pan. Cover the pan with aluminum foil and roast for 20 to 25 minutes, until the peaches are very tender but not mushy. Check after 15 minutes and toss the ingredients before proceeding.

When the peaches are tender, leave them out to cool. When they are soft and roasted, the skins should slip off. This is not necessary, but is easily done if you do not enjoy the texture of peach skins.

To make the candied corn kernels, bring the sugar and water to a boil over medium heat. Scrape out the seeds of the vanilla bean and add them to the sugar-water; put the pod in there, too, for extra flavor. Add the corn kernels to the pot and stir for 15 seconds. Remove the pot from the heat, remove the vanilla pod, and allow to cool.

Whip the remaining 1/2 cup of cream left over from the corn pastry cream recipe and fold into the cooled corn cream.

Cut the cake into 1/2-inch-thick slices.

To build the trifle, spread a thin layer of the corn cream over the bottom of a trifle bowl or decorative glass bowl. Top the cream with pieces of cake to fit snugly, add more cream, peaches, and a sprinkling of candied corn. Fill the bowl until you use up all of your ingredients, probably resulting in 3 full layers of each component. The top layer is up to you—I like to end with a very thin layer of cream fanned with a row of the roasted peaches and a small mound of corn kernels. Refrigerate until ready to serve.

STICKY TOFFEE PUDDING SERVES 8 TO 12

This is a take on a classic English dessert.

Don't let the name *pudding* fool you; the term refers to sweets in England. This recipe is really more of a supermoist caramel cake.

Easy to make and perfect during the holidays, it can be paired with any kind of fall or winter fruit lightly poached or roasted. It also tastes great with ice cream.

CARAMEL SAUCE

2 cups granulated sugar

1 cup heavy cream

CAKE

9 ounces dried, pitted dates, coarsely chopped

¾ cup strong brewed coffee, hot

1 cup plus 2 tablespoons (2¼ sticks) unsalted butter, cut in chunks

1²/3 cups dark brown sugar, lightly packed

6 large eggs

1 tablespoon natural vanilla extract

1²/3 cups all-purpose flour

¾ teaspoon salt

2 teaspoons baking soda

Crème fraîche, for serving (optional)

To make the caramel, in a pot, combine the sugar with ¼ cup of water and heat over medium-low flame; it should look like wet sand. Cook until the sugar melts and begins to caramelize into a syrup, about 5 to 7 minutes. Continue to cook until the sugar begins to boil and takes on a medium amber color, about 3 minutes more. Be careful, the sugar is *really* hot at this point. Remove from the heat and slowly add the cream, a bit at a time, into the hot sugar syrup. It will sputter a bit, so stand back as you pour. When all the bubbling has died down, put the pot back on the burner and bring the mixture to a boil. This will bring together the caramel. Remove the caramel from the heat and set aside to cool slightly.

To make the cake, preheat the oven to 350°F. Coat a 10-inch round cake pan with nonstick spray. Pour 1 cup of the caramel into the pan and rotate it around, so that the caramel sauce completely coats the bottom of the pan. Reserve the remaining caramel sauce at room temperature to serve on the side.

Put the dates in a bowl and pour the hot coffee over them to rehydrate for 10 minutes. While the fruit is soaking, make the rest of the cake batter.

Using a standing electric mixer or hand-held beater, cream the butter and brown sugar until very creamy and light. Add the eggs, 1 at a time, and when they are fully incorporated, add the vanilla. With the addition of the last few eggs, the batter might appear broken. Don't

worry—it will come back together when you add the dry ingredients. Add the flour and salt and continue to mix to combine and give the batter structure.

Put the soaked dates, as well as any coffee left in the bowl, in a food processor or blender. Blend for a minute or 2 to make a fairly smooth puree (it's okay if there are still little chunks of date left). Stir the baking soda into the date puree to dissolve. Mix the date puree into the batter, stirring just to combine; you don't want to overwork the batter.

Pour the cake batter into the caramel-coated pan and spread the surface evenly with a spatula. To bake the cake in a water bath, set the cake pan in a larger roasting pan. Pour very hot water into the roasting pan until the water is about halfway up the sides of the cake pan. Cover the entire roasting pan tightly with foil. Place in the oven to steam the cake for about 1 hour and 15 minutes, until the sides of the cake are firm and springy. If the cake needs longer, cover again and return to the oven. Check the cake every 10 minutes or so.

Remove the cake from the water bath and allow it to cool for about 10 minutes (the cake unmolds better when warm). Run a thin knife around the inside rim of the pan and invert the cake onto a serving dish. Serve warm, with remaining caramel sauce on the side and crème fraîche if desired.

The one requirement of all drinks on the Lever House cocktail list is that they be delicious. They are not overly complicated and don't contain a thousand ingredients. Start with the alcohol, then add a flavoring ingredient and an acid to balance. The bartenders pay special attention to the presentation of the drinks so they look as good as they taste. We make cocktails the classic way, stirring our martinis and using only the best ingredients. All of our syrups and flavorings are made in-house.

Developing the drinks is a team effort between the bar manager, Rainlove Lampariello; the general manager, Steven Eckler; and executive chef Dan Silverman. Whether we are tasting nine different brands of porter or fine-tuning the mix for a new seasonal drink, we are enjoying our work!

COCKTAILS

HUCKLEBERRY FINN SERVES 1

Rain, Lever House's exceptional bartender, won the Grey Goose Taste Maker Contest with this original purple concoction. Its fruity fizz tastes similar to raspberry soda.

2 teaspoons fresh huckleberries
2 ounces (1/4 cup) Grey Goose citron vodka
1 ounce (2 tablespoons) fresh lemon juice
1 ounce (2 tablespoons) Simple Syrup
   (page 234)
Club soda

Using a muddler or the handle of a wooden spoon, smash and crush the huckleberries in a martini shaker or wide glass. Add ice, vodka, lemon juice, and simple syrup; shake it up really well to break the ice into shards. Take the top off of the shaker and pour the contents of the shaker over ice into a Collins glass with all the goodies in there. Fill with club soda.

CITRON LEMONADE SERVES 1

We use all fresh juices in the drinks at Lever House. The cocktails are a group effort: the chef and pastry chef contribute to the ingredients in the bar, sharing the spotlight. The citron lemonade is a spin on a Collins to quench the thirst in the summer.

This refreshing lemonade can easily be made virgin for the kids or mixed with iced tea to make an Arnold Palmer.

10 fresh mint leaves
2 ounces (1/4 cup) Absolut citron vodka
1 1/2 ounces (3 tablespoons) fresh lemon juice
1 ounce (2 tablespoons) Simple Syrup
   (page 234)
Club soda
Lemon wheel, for garnish

Using a muddler or the handle of a wooden spoon, smash and crush the mint in a martini shaker or wide glass to release the natural oils. Add ice, vodka, lemon juice, and simple syrup; shake it up really well to break the ice into shards. Take the top off of the shaker and pour the contents over ice into a Collins glass. Fill with club soda and garnish with lemon.

CALVADOS SIDECAR SERVES 1

The sidecar is one of the most notable cocktails of all time. This interpretation takes the idea and spins it by using apple brandy.

3 ounces (6 tablespoons) Calvados
1 ounce (2 tablespoons) Cointreau
1/2 ounce (1 tablespoon) fresh lemon juice
1/2 ounce (1 tablespoon) fresh lime juice
1/2 ounce (1 tablespoon) Simple Syrup
   (page 234)
1/2 lime
Crushed baked apple chips or sugar in the
   raw, for garnish

Combine the Calvados, Cointreau, lemon juice, lime juice, and simple syrup in a shaker with ice; shake it up really well to break the ice into shards.

Run the lime around the rim of a chilled martini glass to moisten. Rim the glass with the crushed apple chips and strain the drink into it.

This is a take on the famous Italian champagne cocktail and is the most popular signature drink at Lever House. The goal was to transform a standard drink that is usually served during brunch and reinvent it as an evening cocktail with pizzazz.

2$\frac{1}{2}$ ounces (5 tablespoons) Absolut vodka
$\frac{1}{2}$ ounce (1 tablespoon) fresh lime juice
1 ounce (2 tablespoons) peach puree
     or nectar
Champagne
1 paper-thin slice of fresh peach, for garnish

Combine the vodka, lime juice, and peach puree in a shaker with ice, shake it up really well to break the ice into shards. Strain into a chilled martini glass, filling halfway. Float champagne on top and garnish with a slice of peach.

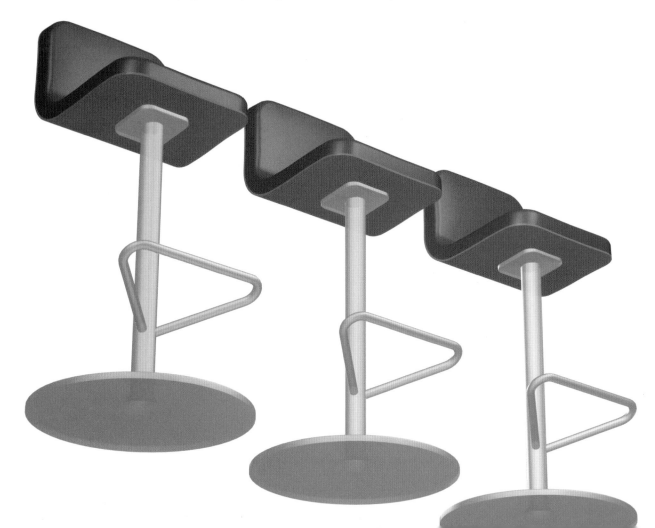

LEFT: CITRON LEMONADE AND BLOOD ORANGE MARTINI

BEES KNEES SERVES 1

BLOOD ORANGE MARTINI SERVES 1

Bees Knees is a classic cocktail hailing from San Francisco. It has subtle aromatic flavor with the essence of juniper. The honey balances out the gin and the lemon juice balances out the honey, all working together to produce a great drink.

Blood oranges are a winter fruit that are breathtakingly vibrant; they create a gorgeous-looking cocktail to be sure. The fruit's viscosity matches well with Stoli, and the Campari gives the drink a dry finish so it is not overly sweet.

3 ounces (6 tablespoons) Junipero gin
1/2 ounce (1 tablespoon) Grand Marnier
1 ounce (2 tablespoons) fresh lemon juice
1 tablespoon honey
1 paper-thin orange slice, for garnish

Combine the gin, Grand Marnier, lemon juice, and honey in a shaker with ice; shake it up really well to break the ice into shards. Strain into a martini glass and garnish with a slice of orange.

3 ounces (6 tablespoons) Stoli Ohranj vodka
1/2 ounce (1 tablespoon) Campari
1/2 ounce (1 tablespoon) fresh lemon juice
1 ounce (2 tablespoons) blood orange juice,
** from 1/2 orange**
1/2 ounce (1 tablespoon) Simple Syrup
** (page 234)**
1 paper-thin blood orange slice, for garnish

Combine the vodka, Campari, lemon juice, blood orange juice, and simple syrup in a shaker with ice; shake it up really well to break the ice into shards. Strain into a martini glass and garnish with a slice of blood orange.

BASICS

The following recipes are not necessarily basic to everything I cook; however, they provide a solid launching pad

to make a meal of restaurant quality. A flavorful stock is one of the most important fundamentals of cooking.

Without a sound base, a dish will be adequate at best, even if you use the most expensive fish or meat. Every

layer of flavor counts to create the sum of the parts.

The concept of basic recipes can cover anything you use repeatedly and that inspires you to pair it with differ-

ent ingredients. There are lots of great vinaigrettes, sauces, and condiments scattered throughout the book that

you can also use to create your own unique combinations. Keep leftovers and put them to use. Play with what you

like and adopt it as part of your arsenal so you can think on your feet come suppertime.

SPICE MIX MAKES ABOUT ¼ CUP

Rub this fragrant spice mix on Venison Carpaccio (page 48), Grilled Short Ribs with Frisée (page 63), and Seared Skate with Roasted Mushrooms, Fingerling Potatoes, and Balsamic-Mushroom Vinaigrette (page 130). This recipe will make a little extra to have around and enjoy.

1 tablespoon juniper berries
1 tablespoon whole black peppercorns
2 tablespoons pink peppercorns
2 tablespoons coriander seeds

Combine the juniper berries, black and pink peppercorns, and coriander seeds in a spice mill or clean coffee grinder; buzz until the spices are a coarse powder. Keep in an airtight container in the cupboard for up to 1 month.

VEGETABLE STOCK MAKES ¾ GALLON

The small amount of salt in this recipe helps draw out flavor from the vegetables as they simmer. A little salt in stock won't reduce down enough to taste overpowering.

2 celery stalks, quartered
2 fennel bulbs, coarsely chopped
1 onion, halved
2 leeks, washed, trimmed, and halved
2 carrots, halved
4 garlic cloves, smashed
2 bay leaves
1 teaspoon whole black peppercorns
6 fresh flat-leaf parsley sprigs
3 fresh thyme sprigs
1 teaspoon kosher salt

In a large stockpot, combine all the ingredients with enough cold water to cover, about 1 gallon. Slowly bring to a boil over medium heat. Reduce the heat to low and gently simmer for 45 minutes, uncovered, skimming any impurities that rise to the surface. Turn off the heat and let the stock steep and settle for 10 minutes. Strain the broth through a fine sieve into another pot to remove the solids. Place the pot in a sink full of ice water and stir to cool the stock down quickly. If not using immediately, cover and refrigerate for up to 1 week or store in the freezer for a month.

BROWN VEAL STOCK MAKES ¾ GALLON

This stock is not all that difficult to make
and is indispensable in a working restaurant
kitchen. Keep it handy always.

2 tablespoons canola oil
5 pounds veal bones, cut into 2-inch chunks,
    preferably meaty leg bones
2 onions, coarsely chopped
1 carrot, coarsely chopped
3 celery stalks, coarsely chopped
Head of garlic, halved
1 leek, coarsely chopped
3 tablespoons tomato paste
1 teaspoon whole black peppercorns
2 bay leaves
3 fresh thyme sprigs

Put a large roasting pan in the oven. Preheat the oven to 425°F. Film the hot pan with the oil and let that heat up in the oven for 2 minutes.

Arrange the veal bones in the pan in a single layer; roast them for 30 to 45 minutes, turning the bones once or twice, until they brown evenly on all sides. Add the vegetables, stir to mix well, and roast for another 10 to 15 minutes, until they brown on the edges. Stir in the tomato paste.

Transfer the bones and onions, carrot, celery, garlic, and leek to a large stockpot. Put the roasting pan on 2 burners over medium-low flame. Pour in 1 cup of water to deglaze the pan and stir with a wooden spoon, scraping to release any caramelized bits that have stuck to the bottom of the pan. Pour this liquid into the stockpot, with enough additional water to cover the ingredients by 1 inch.

Bring the stock to a boil, reduce the heat to low, and gently simmer, uncovered, skimming any impurities that rise to the surface. When no more foam or fat rises to the surface, add the peppercorns, bay leaves, and thyme to the pot. Simmer for 3 to 4 hours, skimming occasionally and adding water as needed to keep the bones and vegetables covered at all times.

Strain the broth through a fine sieve into another pot to remove the solids. Place the pot in a sink full of ice water and stir to cool down the stock quickly. Remove any fat that may solidify on top. If not using immediately, cover and refrigerate for up to 1 week or store in the freezer for a month.

TO MAKE VEAL DEMI-GLACE

Slowly simmer 5 cups of brown veal stock for 1 hour, until the liquid reduces to about a little more than 1 cup. The veal demi-glace should have deep color and be thick enough to coat the back of a spoon. If not using immediately, cover and refrigerate for up to 1 week or store in the freezer for a month.

FISH STOCK/FUMET MAKES 6 CUPS

The delicate white vegetables make a mire-

poix that works well with fish.

**2 to 3 pounds fish bones, from white fish
such as bass, fluke, sole, cod, halibut, etc.
(have at least 1 fish head with gills
removed)**

2 celery stalks, coarsely chopped

1 leek, rinsed well and chopped

1 onion, coarsely chopped

½ fennel bulb, coarsely chopped

1 bay leaf

1 teaspoon whole black peppercorns

1 teaspoon kosher salt

Rinse the fish bones well under cold running
water to remove any impurities. Put the bones
in a stockpot and pour in only enough cold
water to cover by 2 inches; too much will make
the broth taste weak. Slowly bring to a boil,
uncovered, over medium heat, skimming any
foam that rises to the surface. Toss in the vegetables, bay leaf, peppercorns, and salt. When
the stock reaches a boil, reduce the heat to a
simmer and cook gently for 30 minutes.

Turn off the flame and let the stock sit for
15 minutes to cool. Ladle the stock out of the
pot and through a fine strainer into another
pot or container; this removes any sediment.
Place the pot in a sink full of ice water and stir
to cool it down. If not using immediately, cover
and refrigerate for up to 3 days or store in the
freezer for a month.

232 THE LEVER HOUSE COOKBOOK

CHICKEN STOCK MAKES ¾ GALLON

**5 to 6 pounds chicken bones and wings,
    fat trimmed, cut in pieces**
2 onions, coarsely chopped
2 celery stalks, coarsely chopped
1 small carrot, coarsely chopped
1 head of garlic, halved
2 fresh thyme sprigs
1 bay leaf
2 teaspoons whole black peppercorns
1 teaspoon kosher salt

Rinse the chicken bones in cold running water to remove any blood that may adhere to them. Put the bones in a stockpot and pour in only enough cold water to cover by 2 inches; too much will make the broth taste weak. Slowly bring to a boil, uncovered, over medium heat, skimming any foam and fat that rise to the surface. When the stock reaches a boil, reduce the heat to a simmer and toss in the vegetables, herbs, peppercorns, and salt. Continue to simmer gently for about 2 hours, skimming the surface here and there to keep the stock clear and free of fat.

Turn off the flame and let the stock sit for 15 minutes to cool a bit. Strain the stock through a fine sieve into another pot to remove the solids. Place the pot in a sink full of ice water and stir to cool it down. If not using immediately, cover and refrigerate for up to 1 week or store in the freezer for a month.

MUSHROOM JUS MAKES 2 CUPS

**3 pounds button mushrooms, stems
    included, wiped of grit**
½ teaspoon whole black peppercorns
1 bay leaf

Put the mushrooms, peppercorns, and bay leaf in a large stockpot; pour in enough water to generously cover the mushrooms by 2 inches. Bring the stock to a boil, reduce the heat to low, and gently simmer, uncovered, for 2 to 3 hours. The stock should have a pleasant mushroom flavor and have the color of very weak coffee.

Strain the mushroom jus through a fine strainer into another pot to remove the solids, pressing with the back of a wooden spoon to extract as much flavor as possible from the mushrooms. Bring the stock to a boil, and then simmer; reduce by three-quarters to concentrate and enhance the earthy mushroom aroma. If not using immediately, cover and refrigerate for up to 1 week or store in the freezer for a month.

ROASTED GARLIC CONFIT

SIMPLE SYRUP

This confit can be used in the balsamic-mushroom vinaigrette (page 130) and the walnut and garlic tapenade (page 184).

Tender-sweet roasted garlic has a multitude of uses; it keeps in the fridge, and is good with just about anything that garlic fits.

Keep the garlic oil for sautéing potatoes, making vinaigrettes, or brushing on fish before grilling. . . . To make garlic paste, smash the soft garlic cloves in a bowl with a back of a spoon or mash using a knife on a cutting board. Whisk the garlic paste into sauces to thicken without using butter.

1 cup peeled garlic cloves, store-bought
Canola oil, to cover the garlic (about 2 cups)

Preheat the oven to 325°F.

Put the garlic cloves in a single layer in a small baking pan. Pour in enough oil to cover the garlic completely. Cover the pan tightly with aluminum foil and bake for 30 minutes or until the cloves are soft and sort of confit. If they're not quite done after 30 minutes, continue to cook, checking at 5-minute intervals, until the garlic is creamy and completely tender. Be sure that the garlic does not brown, or worse, burn. Cool the roasted garlic in the oil before straining.

1 cup sugar
1 cup water

In a pot over medium heat, combine the sugar and water. Gently simmer for 2 minutes, swirling the pot over the heat now and then, until the sugar is dissolved and the cloudiness of the liquid becomes clear. Do not allow the syrup to boil or get dark.

Cool completely and use to sweeten mixed drinks or iced tea.

SOURCES

chefshop.com has a tremendous range of products, from fleur de sel and Maldon sea salt, to spices such as Aleppo pepper and shichimi togarashi, to luxury items including black truffles and bottarga.

dartagnan.com has a spectrum of goodies, such as poussin, New Zealand venison, foie gras, seasonal wild mushrooms, fresh truffles, and truffle oil.

deananddeluca.com has just about everything, including meats, cheeses, and dry pantry items.

formaggiokitchen.com has a wide array of Italian products, such as saba and fruity extra-virgin olive oils.

gustiamo.com carries extra-virgin olive oils, some cheeses, and anchovies.

kalustyan.com is a great source for exceptionally fragrant dried spices, dried beans, rice, and much more.

nimanranch.com offers all things beef, pork, and lamb. This California-based company is committed to raising animals humanely and sustainably. Their meat is all natural and hormone free, resulting in some of the best-tasting out there. Great pancetta and lardo, too.

sahadis.com has a large selection of Middle Eastern foods, as well as dried fruits, nuts, and olives. Also carries pomegranate molasses.

Salumeria Biellese, salumeriabiellese.com, 212-736-7376 (376 Eighth Avenue 29th Street, New York). Salumeria Biellese has been making all manner of sausages and salamis since 1925. If it is a cured meat product, they have it, including cotechino, lardo, and guanciale. You can view their product list online and then call and order. They ship throughout the United States via FedEx. If you are in New York City, stop by their retail store at the address above.

ACKNOWLEDGMENTS

Writing this book has been a wonderful education. It wouldn't have been possible without the help, inspiration, and participation of many, many people.

I must thank all of the cooks who have ever worked for (or with) me, as well as the prep cooks, dishwashers, and porters. It is their hard work every day and night that makes a restaurant come alive. I would especially like to thank the entire staff of Lever House Restaurant—Steven Eckler, a great friend and general manager; Deborah Snyder, pastry chef extraordinaire; Erik Mongno, executive sous-chef and head cheerleader for team Lever; Mike Cooperman, sous-chef; and all of the managers, cooks, prep people, waiters, bartenders, food runners, dishwashers, and porters. Without you I'm just a guy with a few interesting ideas. . . .

I'd like to acknowledge the inspiration and education these great food writers have provided me over the years: Patience Gray, Elizabeth David, Richard Olney, and Paula Wolfert.

Thank you to Josh Pickard, Robert Nagle, and John McDonald—the owners of Lever House Restaurant.

Thank you to Pam Krauss, Aliza Fogelson, Marysarah Quinn, and the whole Clarkson Potter team; your perceptive comments, intelligent vision, and faith in this book made everything that much easier.

Thanks as well to Lance Reynolds for helping to make the idea of this book a reality and for connecting me with JoAnn Cianciulli, who helped me get it all down on paper, to Barry Wine just because, and to Roberto D'Addona for the great photographs and all the excellent automotive advice.

Thank you to my mother, Eleanor Silverman, one of the most talented, organized, and curious cooks I've ever known. For my father—Dad, I wish you were here to read this book.

Last, but certainly not least, a huge thank you to my wife, Susan, whose trust, faith, patience, sense of humor, and confidence continue to inspire me. And for Georgia, who's just starting to cook. I love you both.

—DAN SILVERMAN

Writing cookbooks for a living is quite possibly the most fulfilling job on the planet. I love what I do and am so appreciative for the bounty of blessings that have come my way. Bringing the menu of Lever House Restaurant to life has been an extraordinary experience. This book would not have been possible without the intelligence and loyalty of my coauthor, superstar chef Dan Silverman. Dan, thank you for inviting me into your inner sanctum and for teaching me so many cool things about food. You are a great professional mentor and it has been a true joy to work with you on countless levels.

Much appreciation to pastry chef Deborah Snyder and mixologist Rainlove Lampariello for their passion and precision in creating some of the best desserts and cocktails in New York. Thank you for sharing your secrets.

Props to Roberto D'Addona for your vibrant photographs that effectively capture the glory and spirit of Lever House.

Thanks to the dapper gentlemen of Lever House Restaurant, Josh Pickard, Robert Nagle, John McDonald, and Steven Eckler, who always treat me like family.

To the indefatigable Lance Reynolds, thank you for cultivating this project and for graciously supporting me throughout. Chook, you're a class act and esteemed friend.

Special thanks to the omnipotent Pam Krauss at Clarkson Potter, a spectacular woman who is as savvy as they come. I have the utmost respect for you.

Thank you to our skillful editor, Aliza Fogelson, for your guidance, insight, and patience. This is a better book because of you.

Thanks to Bob Stein, who mastered all the legal stuff so we could get cooking.

I would like to acknowledge my father, Dominic, who took me out to dinner from an early age and taught me how to eat in a restaurant. I hope you are proud of me.

—JOANN CIANCIULLI